Anonymous

Poetical Tributes to the Memory of Abraham Lincoln

Anonymous

Poetical Tributes to the Memory of Abraham Lincoln

ISBN/EAN: 9783337777616

Printed in Europe, USA, Canada, Australia, Japan

Cover: Foto ©Thomas Meinert / pixelio.de

More available books at **www.hansebooks.com**

L. L. Bowen,
Woodstock, Vt.

Oct, 31st 1865

POETICAL TRIBUTES

TO THE

MEMORY OF

ABRAHAM LINCOLN.

PHILADELPHIA
J. B. LIPPINCOTT & CO.
1865.

IN GOD IS OUR TRUST.

"Peace to the just man's memory,—let it grow
    Greener with years, and blossom through the flight
Of ages: let the mimic canvass show
    His calm benevolent features; let the light
    Stream on his deeds of love, that shunned the sight
Of all but Heaven; and in the book of fame,
    The glorious record of his virtues write,
And hold it up to men, and bid them claim
A palm like his, and catch from him the hallowed flame."

INTRODUCTION.

IN the preparation of this volume it has been the purpose of the publishers to preserve, in permanent form, the spontaneous tributes of esteem and affection tendered to the memory of our late beloved President by the poetical writers of our own and other countries. It seems especially fitting that the tender regard which Mr. Lincoln had won for himself during the four eventful years of his Presidency, and which has found so many and such heartfelt expressions since his untimely death, should have a lasting record; and both for the gratification of those who have mingled their tears over the remains of the illustrious dead, and as an evidence to future generations of how wise and great and good we thought him, this volume is now put forth.

PHILADELPHIA, *July* 1, 1865.

INDEX.

	PAGE
ANONYMOUS................."Dies Iræ".........................	44
ADAMS, GEORGE...	95
A——, S..	103
ANONYMOUS...................English Paper.................	130
ANONYMOUS..............." Sic Semper Tyrannis"........	196
ANONYMOUS..................."Gone"............................	242
ANONYMOUS...................Montreal, Canada............	260
ANCKER, ADOLPH..	276
ANONYMOUS...........20, 22, 55, 77, 91, 97, 99, 100, 107, 132, 164, 177, 189, 197	
201, 208, 216, 229, 260, 269, 270, 278, 282, 284, 285, 292, 299	
BRYANT, WM. CULLEN...................................	13
BALLARD, H. C...	21
BARNETT, J. G..	58
BENSON, JOHN S...	109
BENJAMIN, S. G. W...	110
BEALE, Mrs. O. A. S..	119
BICKERSTAFF, Miss EMMA H....." Columbia's Lament".........	129
BOYLAN, WM..	256
B——, C. R...	272
BENNETT, EMMA BENTON...............................	277
CHITTENDEN, RICHARD HENRY.......................	34
CARY, PHŒBE...	37

(vii)

INDEX.

	PAGE
CARY, ALICE............"Inscribed to London Punch"............	53
CROMWELL, RUTH N..	121
COOPER, GEO..	124
C——, C..	145
COX, CHRISTOPHER C..	149
CIST, L. J..................St. Louis, Mo..................	155
COLLINS, JOHN..	159
CAMERON, Mrs. R. A.......... { "Ours the Cross, Thine the Crown." Brashear City, Texas. }	171
CRANCH, C. P..	214
CARRIE,..	240
CLARK, Rev. ALEX..	257
COOLBRITH, INA D..............San Francisco..................	262
DUNN, CALEB..	45
DUGANNE, A. J. H..	59
DYER, Rev. SIDNEY..	117
DORSEY, DENNIS B..	163
DEMBY, ANGELINE R..	220
DENNISON, MARY A..........."To Mrs. Lincoln"............	222
D——, S. J..	237
DAVIS, D. AMBROSE..	286
DAWES, L. M..	303
EMISSUS.................."To Mrs. Lincoln"............	81
ETA..	85
EVANS, ALBERT S..	87
EVA..	87
EMMA..	186
ENOLA..	290
FIELD, J. A..	79
FISHER, JABEZ M..	123
FAVORITE, FLORY..	162
FIELD, J. G..	173
FAIRFIELD, P. G..	211

INDEX.

	PAGE
F———, BELLE	231
F———, L. W.	265
"FUN," FROM THE LONDON	292
G———, JEANIE............"De Profundis"	105
G———, C. D.	108
GREENWOOD, Rev. T. J.	116
GERTRUDE	188
GRIFFIN, F. P.	280
GURLEY, Rev. Dr. D. P.	305
HOWE, Mrs. JULIA WARD	15
HOOPER, Mrs. LUCY HAMILTON	25 and 74
HAYWARD, J. HENRY	60
HALPINE, CHARLES G..........." Miles O'Reilly"	62
HOPPER, Rev. EDWARD	64
HOLMES, OLIVER WENDELL	73
HOSMER, W. H. C.	76
HALL, Mrs. F. W...............Seventy years of age	125
H———, A. E.	185
HARTZ, MARY E.	223
HIRST, HENRY B.	251
H———, S. B.	253
HALPINE, M. G.	259
IOLA	89
J———, L. H.	194
JOHNSON, R. M.	255
KIMBALL, HARRIET McEWEN	42
LAIGHTON, ALBERT	83
LEECH, HARRY HAREWOOD	133
LAWSON, EMILIE............San Francisco	174
LOWE, MARTHA PERRY	205
LEAH...............New Orleans	249

INDEX.

	PAGE
L———, H. A.	254
LISLE, CORA	287
MACKELLAR, THOMAS	16
MERREFIELD, JOSEPH	49
MORFORD, HENRY	69
MUNDAY, EUGENIE H......"A Crime without a Name"	72
MORGAN, GEORGE G. W.	98
MANLOVE, OLIVER PERRY	102
McBOYLE, A.	109
"MAY" OF SPARROWBUSH......Thirteen years of age	127
MARTIN, G......Montreal, Canada	153 and 180
McL———, J.	213
MEREDITH, GULA	250
McCAFFREY, Miss S. A.	275
MERCER, S. C.	295
McMILLAN'S MAGAZINE......England	301
N———, F. L.	184
NICHOLS, KATE W.	264
NOWELL, EDWARD P.	271
NICHOL, JOHN......London Spectator	302
PROCTOR, EDNA DEAN	40
PUNCH, FROM THE LONDON	50
P———, E. B.	84
PRINCE, Rev. N. A.	104
P———, ...New Orleans	131
PYMN, HENRY	134
PEREGRINATOR......California	152
PHELPS, Rev. Dr. S. D.	200
PARKER, B. S.	225
RAENHART, GEO. W.	56
REMAK, Mrs. GUSTAVUS	114
RICHARDSON, Mrs. M. T. G.	137
RISTINE, JAMES	168

INDEX. xi

	PAGE
REED, CHARLES W..	175
ROSARR, ELLERTON...............Montreal, Canada.....................	204
ROBINSON, Mrs. J. T..	207
ROBBINS..	234
R———, E. V...	235
RADFORD, BEN. J..	243
REXFORD, EBEN E..	246
STEDMAN, EDMUND C..............." Sonnet "...............................	17
SCHERB, EMANUEL VITALIS..	18
STODDARD, RICHARD HENRY...." An Horatian Ode ".................	27
SMITH, EMELINE SHERMAN..46 and 148
S———, H. S..	106
STOCKTON, D. D., Rev. THOMAS H...	144
STEWART, JAMES M	167
S———, E. V...	191
S———, G. F...	206
S———, JENNIE E..	209
STEBBINS, Mrs. C. M..	215
SHIRLEY..	233
ST. CLAIR, WINNIFRED...	244
S———, E. T..................." To the Nation "...............................	287
TUCKERMAN, HENRY T...	24
TAYLOR, B. F...	93
TOWNSEND, GEO. ALFRED...	141
TAYLOR, BENJAMIN FRANKLIN.." The President's Dream "........	267
UNA...	178
UMBRA..	258
UPHAM, NATHAN...	283
V———, M. V...	139
VANDENHOFF, GEO................." Treason's Masterpiece "............	158
WILLIS, RICHARD STORRS...14 and 92
WOODWORTH, H..	143
W———, E. J...	227

	PAGE
WHITE, JOSEPHINE	230
WARD, THOMAS	273
WHITING, SAM	274
WILLIAMS, Mrs. L. M.	281
W———, R. B.	288
WEBB, C. H.................San Francisco	298

POETICAL TRIBUTES

TO THE

MEMORY OF ABRAHAM LINCOLN.

By WILLIAM CULLEN BRYANT.

O, SLOW to smite and swift to spare,
  Gentle and merciful and just!
Who, in the fear of God, didst bear
  The sword of power—a nation's trust.

In sorrow by thy bier we stand,
  Amid the awe that hushes all,
And speak the anguish of a land
  That shook with horror at thy fall.

Thy task is done—the bond are free;
  We bear thee to an honored grave,
Whose noblest monument shall be
  The broken fetters of the slave.

Pure was thy life; its bloody close
  Hath placed thee with the sons of light,
Among the noble host of those
  Who perished in the cause of right.

By RICHARD STORRS WILLIS.

REGRETFUL bells are tolling,
With mournful knell profound;
Unwilling guns are booming,
With dull and solemn sound!
  A pilgrim chief is passing
  From 'neath the nation's dome,
  To find from life's sad labors
  A resting-place, at home!
Home, home, sweet, sweet home!
For all the worn and weary,
There's no place like home!

And fevered hearts are throbbing,
Right royal hearts and true!
And fitful tears are starting
From eyes where tears are few!
  That pilgrim chief's a martyr,
  Who fell the State to save!
  The home that he is seeking,
  The martyred patriot's grave!
Home, home, sweet, sweet home!
For thee, O martyred patriot,
There's no place like home!

Now open wide thy portals,
Thou proud and prairied West!
And decked with Spring's bright verdure,
Take LINCOLN to thy breast!

Sing, birds, his Miserere!
Ye grasses, lightly wave!
And you, ye shades of heroes,
  Glide forth, and guard his grave!
Home, home, sweet, sweet home!
Sleep well, thou martyred chieftain—
There's no place like home!

The light is breaking o'er us,
And Treason sinks appalled!
Arise! redeemed Columbia!
Thy land is disenthralled!
  And though the good man perish,
  From out his hallowed dust
  Forth springs a race of heroes,
  To guard the same high trust!
Home, home, sweet, sweet home
We'll evermore defend it—
There's no place like home!

By Mrs. JULIA WARD HOWE.

CROWN his blood-stained pillow
  With a victor's palm;
Life's receding billow
  Leaves eternal calm.

At the feet Almighty
  Lay this gift sincere;
Of a purpose weighty,
  And a record clear.

With deliverance freighted
　Was this passive hand,
And this heart, high-fated,
　Would with love command.

Let him rest serenely
　In a Nation's care,
Where her waters queenly
　Make the West most fair.

In the greenest meadow
　That the prairies show,
Let his marble's shadow
　Give all men to know:

"Our First Hero, living,
　Made his country free;
Heed the Second's giving,
　Death for Liberty."

By THOMAS MACKELLAR.

SO deep our grief, it may be silence is
　　The meetest tribute to the father's name:
A secret shrine in every breast is his,
　Whom death hath girt with an immortal fame;
And in this dim recess our thoughts abide,
　Clad in the garment of unspoken grief,
As fain the sorrow of the heart to hide
　That yields no tears to give our wo relief.

"But death is not to such as he," we sigh;
"His heart is still—his pulse may beat no more;
Yet men so good and loved do never die;
 But while the tide shall flow upon the shore
Of time to come, a presence to the eye
 Of nations shall he be, and evermore
Shall freemen treasure in historic page
The martyr-hero of earth's noblest age."

SONNET.

By EDMUND C. STEDMAN.

"FORGIVE them, for they know not what they do!"
 He said, and so went shriven to his fate—
Unknowing went, that generous heart and true.
 Even while he spoke, the slayer lay in wait,
 And when the morning opened Heaven's gate,
There passed the whitest soul a nation knew.
 Henceforth all thoughts of pardon are too late;
They, in whose cause that arm its weapon drew,
 Have murdered MERCY. Now alone shall stand
Blind JUSTICE, with the sword unsheathed she wore.
 Hark, from the Eastern to the Western strand,
The swelling thunder of the people's roar:
 What words they murmur—FETTER NOT HER HAND!
SO LET IT SMITE; SUCH DEEDS SHALL BE NO MORE!

By EMMANUEL VITALIS SCHERB.

OH woe! oh woe! oh woe!
What awful sudden blow
Has changed to funeral moans our songs of exultation!
But yesterday so bright,
To-day in darkest night
Are quenched the blazing lights of joy's illumination.
We stagger to and fro,
Ourselves struck by the blow
Of this most vile, most foul, most fell assassination.
The truth to credit slow,
We ask: *Can* it be so?
Is he indeed laid low,
The ruler wise, and firm, and faithful, of this nation?

Oh grievous, grievous loss!
Oh heavy, heavy cross!
This orphaned nation's heart is tottering, reeling under!
From a smiling azure sky,
In the twinkling of an eye,
Down crashed the fearful bolt that cleft our Head asunder.
Alas! now prostrate lies
That chief so calm and wise,
Alike for goodness famed, for strength and moderation;
With eyes that tears bedim,
With hearts full to the brim,
We lose, we mourn in him,
Alike with Washington, a Father of this Nation.

Oh horrid, horrid crime,
Bred in the foulest slime
Of·Slavery's loathsome pool, all rotting with stagnation!
Oh dastard, dastard crime,
Unheard of in this clime,
Where men wage open *war*, but scorn *assassination*.
Oh senseless, senseless crime,
Committed at a time
Of reawakening hopes of peace and conciliation!
Alas! what dost thou gain?
In fury blind, insane,
The *mild* one thou hast slain.
A *sterner* now will reign,
And thou hast roused again
The slumbering thunderbolts of Wrath's retaliation.

But, nation deeply bowed,
Be all thy grief allowed,
Allowed be too thy wrath, thy righteous indignation!
But, like thy martyred chief,
Temper thy wrath and grief
With noble self-control and generous moderation.
Be just! give each his due,
Let those be slain who slew,
Be blood for blood the fair and lawful reparation!
But, Justice satisfied,
Let Wisdom be thy guide,
Keep Mercy at thy side,
Finish thy sacred task, *our Union's restoration!*

Then from the firmament
Will he whom we lament,

Our nation's martyred saint,
Wearing a golden crown,
Benignantly look down,
And let his blessing rest for aye upon his nation.

ANONYMOUS.

GRIEF-PIERCED unto her great heart's core,
Bowed to the dust and stricken sore,
The Nation leaves her task undone
To weep in anguish o'er a son
Whom she shall see no more, no more.

Proudly, a few short hours before,
Exulting in her joy, she bore
Aloft her starry flag—her brow
Aglow with victory: and now
She sits and moans, "No more! no more!"

No vengeance on the wretch who tore
Her loved one from her, can restore
The life she prized—though wrathful, grim,
She seize and rend him limb from limb—
The lost returns no more, no more!

Too just to wrong, too meek to soar,
His heart was of the sterling ore:
Not proudly strong, but grandly pure.
He saw his crowning work mature
In triumph; then—no more, no more.

Honored in life, in death he wore
The crown of martyrdom, and o'er
The witness of his life there glows
The lurid grandeur of its close,
To light the ages evermore.

By H. C. BALLARD.

WHY, why, O God! this sorrow sent,
This grief that fills the continent?
Why droops our noble flag to-day?
All hearts feel sadness and dismay—
For he who held with faithful hand
The welfare of this mighty land,
Rests now in death's heroic sleep,
While gloom prevails and millions weep.

Oh! grief no human tongue can tell—
As if God's fearful judgment-bell
From out the midnight sky had hurled
His wrath upon a sleeping world!
We tremble that this act of crime
Should stain the annals of our time—
That one should live whose guilty hand
Could smite the saviour of our land!

How sudden fell the cruel blow
That laid our noble leader low—
Our hearts were full of blissful cheer,
We saw the dawn of peace draw near!

We prayed that he whose honest hand
Had toiled to save this free-born land,
Might live to bear the honors won
From duty well and nobly done.

Know ye, who nerved the bloody hand
That fills with gloom our native land,
That he who rests in death's embrace
Looked kindly on your guilty race!
Now may the godless traitors feel
How deep can go the freeman's steel!
Let mercy lose its gentle power,
And God's stern justice rule the hour!

Though dead, he lives in endless fame—
All honor to his patriot name;
All glory, for his loyal hand
Gave freedom to our mountain land!
That priceless boon shall ever be
The pride and glory of the free;
And LINCOLN's fame grow brighter yet,
Till Time's remotest sun shall set.

ANONYMOUS.

ACROSS the heights of future time,
To all true men of every clime
One name will swell, a sound sublime.

Our children, 'neath a prosperous sun,
Peace, Law, and Right all blent in one,
Will own his glorious mission done—

Will say, true hearts speak out who can.
There rose a cry, God shaped his plan;
He ruled events, he sent the man.

A man who held the Nation's trust;
Pure gold, where much was dross and dust.
No tears above his honored dust.

Our heart this shining memory wears
To bliss-like deep, unspoken prayers,
To make us strong 'midst daily cares.

He said to every slave, "Go free!
To God—no other—bend the knee;
His glorious bidding speaks through me."

No selfish thought, no blinding pride;
His vision clear, his soul stood wide
To God, and all the world beside!

Triumphant will their voices ring!
Glad tribute to his truth we bring!
Speak, men, his praise! ye poets, sing!

Ah me! with trembling voice instead,
With sorrowing hearts, with drooping head,
We cry, "Our Martyr Friend is dead!"

By HENRY T. TUCKERMAN.

SHROUD the Banner! rear the Cross!
Consecrate a Nation's loss;
Gaze on that majestic sleep,
Stand beside the bier to weep;
Lay the gentle son of toil
Proudly in his native soil;
Crowned with honor, to his rest
Bear the Prophet of the West!

How cold the brow that yet doth wear
The impress of a Nation's care;
How still the heart whose every beat
Glowed with compassion's sacred heat;
Rigid the lips whose patient smile
Duty's stern task would oft beguile;
Blood-quenched the pensive eye's soft light,
Nerveless the hand so loath to smite,
So meek in rule, it leads, though dead,
The People as in life it led.

O! let his wise and guileless sway
Win every recreant to-day,
And sorrow's vast and holy wave
Blend all our hearts around his grave!
Let the faithful bondsmen's tears,
Let the traitor's craven fears,
And the people's grief and pride
Plead against the parricide!

Let us throng to pledge and pray
O'er the patriot-martyr's clay;
Then with solemn faith in right,
That made him victor in the fight,
Cling to the path he fearless trod,
Still radiant with the smile of God.

Shroud the Banner! rear the Cross!
Consecrate a Nation's loss!
Gaze on that majestic sleep,
Stand beside the bier to weep;
Lay the gentle son of toil
Proudly in his native soil;
Crowned with honor, to his rest
Bear the Prophet of the West!

By Mrs. LUCY HAMILTON HOOPER.

THERE is a shadow on the sunny air,
   There is a darkness o'er the April day,
We bow our heads beneath this awful cloud
   So sudden come, and not to pass away.

O the wild grief that sweeps across our land
   From frozen Maine to Californian shore!
A people's tears, an orphaned nation's wail,
   For him the good, the great, who is no more.

The noblest brain that ever toiled for man,
   The kindest heart that ever thrilled a breast,
The lofty soul unstained by soil of earth,
   Sent by a traitor to a martyr's rest.

And his last act (O gentle, kindly heart!)
    The noble prompting of unselfish grace.
He would not disappoint the waiting crowd
    Who came to gaze upon his honored face.

O God, thy ways are just, and yet we find
    This dispensation hard to understand
Why must our Prophet's weary feet be stay'd
    Upon the borders of the Promised Land?

He bore the heat, the burden of the day,
    The golden eventide he shall not see;
He shall not see the old flag wave again
    Over a land united, saved, and free.

He loved his people, and he ever lent
    To all our griefs a sympathizing ear;
Now for the first time in these four sad years
    The stricken nation wails—he does not hear.

O never wept a land a nobler Chief!
    Kind heart, strong hand, true soul—yet while we weep,
Let us remember, e'en amid our tears,
    'Tis God who gives to his beloved sleep.

So sleeps he now, the chosen man of God,
    No more shall care or sorrow wring his breast;
The weary one and heavy-laden, lies
    Hushed by the voice of God to endless rest.

We need no solemn knell, no tolling bells,
    No chanted dirge, no vain words sadly said.
The saddest knell that ever stirred the air
    Rang in those words, "Our President is dead!"

AN HORATIAN ODE.

By RICHARD HENRY STODDARD.

By Special Permission of the Publishers, Messrs. Bunce & Huntington.

NOT as when some great captain falls
In battle, where his country calls,
    Beyond the struggling lines
    That push his dread designs

To doom, by some stray ball struck dead:
Or, in the last charge, at the head
    Of his determined men,
    Who must be victors then!

Nor as when sink the civic great,
The safer pillars of the State,
    Whose calm, mature, wise words
    Suppress the need of swords!—

With no such tears as e'er were shed
Above the noblest of our dead
    Do we to-day deplore
    The man that is no more!

Our sorrow hath a wider scope,
Too strange for fear, too vast for hope,—
    A wonder, blind and dumb,
    That waits—what is to come!

Not more astounded had we been
If madness, that dark night, unseen,
  Had in our chambers crept,
  And murdered while we slept!

We woke to find a mourning earth—
Our Lares shivered on the hearth,—
  The roof-tree fallen,—all
  That could affright, appall!

Such thunderbolts, in other lands,
Have smitten the rod from royal hands,
  But spared, with us, till now,
  Each laurelled Cesar's brow!

No Cesar he, whom we lament,
A man without a precedent,
  Sent it would seem, to do
  His work—and perish too!

Not by the weary cares of state,
The endless tasks, which will not wait,
  Which, often done in vain,
  Must yet be done again:

Not in the dark, wild tide of war,
Which rose so high, and rolled so far,
  Sweeping from sea to sea
  In awful anarchy:—

Four fateful years of mortal strife,
Which slowly drained the nation's life,
  (Yet, for each drop that ran
  There sprang an armed man!).

Not then;—but when by measures meet,—
By victory, and by defeat,—
    By courage, patience, skill,
    The people's fixed "We will!"

Had pierced, had crushed rebellion dead,—
Without a hand, without a head:—
    At last, when all was well,
    He fell—O, how he fell!

The time,—the place,—the stealing shape,—
The coward shot,—the swift escape,—
    The wife—the widow's scream,—
    It is a hideous dream!

A dream?—what means this pageant, then?
These multitudes of solemn men,
    Who speak not when they meet,
    But throng the silent street?

The flags half-mast, that late so high
Flaunted at each new victory?
    (The stars no brightness shed,
    But bloody looks the red!)

The black festoons that stretch for miles,
And turn the streets to funeral aisles?
    (No house too poor to show
    The nation's badge of woe!)

The cannon's sudden, sullen boom,—
The bells that toll of death and doom,—
    The rolling of the drums,—
    The dreadful car that comes?

Cursed be the hand that fired the shot!
The frenzied brain that hatched the plot!
  Thy country's father slain
  By thee, thou worse than Cain!

Tyrants have fallen by such as thou,
And good hath followed—may it now!
  (God lets bad instruments
  Produce the best events.)

But he, the man we mourn to-day,
No tyrant was: so mild a sway
  In one such weight who bore
  Was never known before!

Cool should he be, of balanced powers,
The ruler of a race like ours,
  Impatient, headstrong, wild,—
  The man to guide the child!

And this he was, who most unfit
(So hard the sense of God to hit!)
  Did seem to fill his place.
  With such a homely face,—

Such rustic manners,—speech uncouth,—
(That somehow blundered out the truth!)
  Untried, untrained to bear
  The more than kingly care!

Ay! And his genius put to scorn
The proudest in the purple born,
  Whose wisdom never grew
  To what, untaught, he knew—

The people, of whom he was one.
No gentleman like Washington,—
 (Whose bones, methinks, make room,
 To have him in their tomb!)

A laboring man, with horny hands,
Who swung the axe, who tilled his lands,
 Who shrank from nothing new,
 But did as poor men do!

One of the people! Born to be
Their curious epitome;
 To share, yet rise above
 Their shifting hate and love.

Common his mind (it seemed so then),
His thoughts the thoughts of other men:
 Plain were his words, and poor—
 But now they will endure!

No hasty fool, of stubborn will,
But prudent, cautious, pliant, still;
 Who, since his work was good,
 Would do it, as he could.

Doubting, was not ashamed to doubt,
And, lacking prescience, went without:
 Often appeared to halt,
 And was, of course, at fault:

Heard all opinions, nothing loth,
And loving both sides, angered both:
 Was—not like justice, blind,
 But watchful, clement, kind.

No hero, this, of Roman mould;
Nor like our stately sires of old:
    Perhaps he was not great—
    But he preserved the State!

O honest face, which all men knew!
O tender heart, but known to few!
    O wonder of the age,
    Cut off by tragic rage!

Peace! Let the long procession come,
For hark!—the mournful, muffled drum—
    The trumpet's wail afar,—
    And see! the awful car!

Peace! Let the sad procession go,
While cannon boom, and bells toll slow:
    And go, thou sacred car,
    Bearing our woe afar!

Go, darkly borne, from State to State,
Whose loyal, sorrowing cities wait
    To honor all they can
    The dust of that good man!

Go, grandly borne, with such a train
As greatest kings might die to gain:
    The just, the wise, the brave
    Attend thee to the grave!

And you, the soldiers of our wars,
Bronzed veterans, grim with noble scars,
    Salute him once again,
    Your late commander—slain!

Yes, let your tears, indignant, fall,
But leave your muskets on the wall:
    Your country needs you now
    Beside the forge, the plough!

(When justice shall unsheathe her brand,—
If mercy may not stay her hand,
    Nor would we have it so—
    She must direct the blow!)

And you, amid the master-race,
Who seem so strangely out of place,
    Know ye who cometh? He
    Who hath declared ye free!

Bow while the body passes—nay,
Fall on your knees, and weep, and pray!
    Weep, weep—I would ye might—
    Your poor, black faces white!

And, children, you must come in bands,
With garlands in your little hands,
    Of blue, and white, and red,
    To strew before the dead!

So, sweetly, sadly, sternly goes
The fallen to his last repose:
    Beneath no mighty dome,
    But in his modest home;

The churchyard where his children rest,
The quiet spot that suits him best:
    There shall his grave be made,
    And there his bones be laid!

And there his countrymen shall come,
With memory proud, with pity dumb,
    And strangers far and near,
    For many and many a year!

For many a year, and many an age,
While history on her ample page
    The virtues shall enroll
    Of that paternal soul!

By RICHARD H. CHITTENDEN.

ALAS! what mean these sights and sounds of woe!
    The sable drapery and tolling bell!
Men mutely gazing at each other on
The street, with lips compressed and firm set teeth
And faces pale with speechless rage and fear,
And horror inexpressible! How changed!
But yesterday, and every mast and spire
Put forth our glorious banner to the breeze
And blossomed in the sun of victory!
What fatal frost in one short night, this blight
Hath wrought! Hast heard it not? Lincoln is dead!
Assassinated at the Capital!
By Treason, slain in triumph's supreme hour!
Ah, what a plunge from loftiest height of joy
Deep down into this dark abyss of grief!
Then weep, strong man, be not ashamed of tears!
Weep, gentle woman, for his honest heart,
So kind and true, is silent evermore!

Earth seems to mourn, and Heaven in tearful showers
Laments the fall of Freedom's noblest son;
This day was slain our Lord to save a world!*
And thou art slain a nation's sacrifice!
Columbia, lay aside thy festal robes
And hide thy tears in woe's habiliments!
The laurel to the cypress yield; the song
Of victory, to the tearful dirge: O God!
Why must thy chosen ones be martyrs still!

Freedom's Messiah whom we late have learned
To know and love, could'st thou no longer spare?
Whom thou, like David, for thy work, didst call
To grapple with our giant foe! obscure,
Unknown, our champion came, and little skilled
In sophistry, but yet in honesty
Invincible! He fought and victor died!
Hast thou not set upon his head the crown
Of martyrdom lest some untoward step
The lustre of his spotless fame might dim?
'Tis well! Lest treason might not die, he died!
Your only hope ye've slain, Confederates;
Now shall ye drink the dregs of penalty!
Our martyr head; our Moses, who hast led
This undeserving people safely through
The wilderness of war unto the promised land
Of peace! Thank God thou wert not sooner called!
That thou, like Israel's chief on Nebo's top,
Didst live to see the old flag floating from
  Proud Richmond's towers; the dawning of the day!

* Good Friday.

And Slavery's ranks in terror melt away
Before the charge of Freedom's gallant sons.
Immortal infamy is won, foul fiend!
For hell, astounded at this damned crime,
Nor name for it, nor place for thee can find.
Go, wander up and down! Cain's mark is thine!
Escape, if from thyself thou canst escape!
A million argus eyes are on thee, and
A million swords shall from their scabbards leap
To rid the Earth of those who thee defend;
Preach, minions, if ye dare, apology
For treason unto loyal ears; your day
Is past; the lion of the North is roused;
And since ye proudly scorned mercy's hand,
And as that gentle hand its boon held forth,
Struck down at once the giver and the gift,
So shall ye die; for where he fell stands one
Who will avenge him; one who calls crime, crime;
Nor weakly counts him less a murderer, who
Ten thousand kills God's image to enslave,
Than he who in his quarrel slays but one!
The blood of twice one hundred thousand braves
From gory battle fields and graves unknown,
And thousands more, whom God in mercy took
From prison pens and dire starvation, to
The assembly of the heroic dead above,
And unborn heirs of Lincoln's deathless name,
And outraged Justice in her thunder tones,
Cry vengeance, vengeance on those parricides!
Vengeance is mine, I will repay, saith God;

But are not men his chosen instruments?
No longer miscreants our land pollute!
But straightway take your bloody stains to Him,
Whose just omnipotence perchance may find
A punishment to match your infinite guilt!
Lincoln! nor marble shaft, nor storied urn
We need thy memory to perpetuate!
Thy name on every loyal heart's engraved!
Thy monument shall be thy country saved,
Thy epitaph: Here lies an honest man.

By PHŒBE CARY.

OUR sun hath gone down at the noonday,
    The heavens are black;
And over the morning the shadows
    Of night-time are back.

Stop the proud boasting mouth of the cannon,
    Hush the mirth and the shout;—
God is God! and the ways of Jehovah
    Are past finding out.

Lo! the beautiful feet on the mountains,
    That yesterday stood;
The white feet that came with glad tidings,
    Are dabbled in blood.

The Nation that firmly was settling
    The crown on her head,

Sits, like Rizpah, in sackcloth and ashes,
    And watches her dead.

Who is dead? who, unmoved by our wailing,
    Is lying so low?
O, my Land, stricken dumb in your anguish,
    Do you feel, do you know,

That the hand which reached out of the darkness
    Hath taken the whole?
Yea, the arm and the head of the people—
    The heart and the soul!

And that heart, o'er whose dread awful silence
    A nation has wept;
Was the truest, and gentlest, and sweetest,
    A man ever kept!

Once this good man, we mourn, overwearied,
    Worn, anxious, oppressed,
Was going out from his audience chamber
    For a season to rest;

Unheeding the thousands who waited
    To honor and greet,
When the cry of a child smote upon him,
    And turned back his feet.

"Three days hath a woman been waiting,"
    Said they, "patient and meek."
And he answered, "Whatever her errand,
    Let me hear; let her speak!"

So she came, and stood trembling before him,
    And pleaded her cause;
Told him all; how her child's erring father
    Had broken the laws.

Humbly spake she: "I mourn for his folly,
    His weakness, his fall;"
Proudly spake she: "he is not a TRAITOR,
    And I love him through all!"

Then the great man, whose heart had been shaken
    By a little babe's cry;
Answered soft, taking counsel of mercy,
    "This man shall not die!"

Why, he heard from the dungeons, the rice-fields,
    The dark holds of ships;
Every faint, feeble cry which oppression
    Smothered down on men's lips.

In her furnace, the centuries had welded
    Their fetter and chain;
And like withes, in the hands of his purpose,
    He snapped them in twain.

Who can be what he was to the people;
    What he was to the State?
Shall the ages bring to us another
    As good, and as great?

Our hearts with their anguish are broken,
    Our wet eyes are dim;

For us is the loss and the sorrow,
    The triumph for him!

For, ere this, face to face with his Father
    Our Martyr hath stood;
Giving into his hand the white record,
    With its great seal of blood!

By EDNA DEAN PROCTOR.

NOW must the storied Potomac
    Laurels for ever divide,
Now to the Sangamon fameless
    Give of its century's pride.
Sangamon, stream of the prairies,
    Placidly westward that flows,
Far in whose city of silence
    Calm he has sought his repose.
Over our Washington's river
    Sunrise beams rosy and fair,
Sunset on Sangamon fairer—
    Father and martyr lies there.

Kings under pyramids slumber,
    Sealed in the Lybian sands;
Princes in gorgeous cathedrals
    Decked with the spoil of the lands.
Kinglier, princelier sleeps he
    Couched 'mid the prairies serene,
Only the turf and the willow
    Him and God's heaven between!

Temple nor column to cumber
  Verdure and bloom of the sod—
So, in the vale by Beth-peor,
  Moses was buried of God.

Break into blossom, O prairies!
  Snowy and golden and red;
Peers of the Palestine lilies
  Heap for your glorious dead!
Roses as fair as of Sharon,
  Branches as stately as palm,
Odors as rich as the spices—
  Cassia and aloes and balm—
Mary the loved and Salome,
  All with a gracious accord,
Ere the first glow of the morning
  Brought to the tomb of the Lord

Wind of the West! breathe around him
  Soft as the saddened air's sigh
When to the summit of Pisgah
  Moses had journeyed to die.
Clear as its anthem that floated
  Wide o'er the Moabite plain,
Low with the wail of the people
  Blending its burdened refrain.
Rarer, O Wind! and diviner,—
  Sweet as the breeze that went by
When, over Olivet's mountain,
  Jesus was lost in the sky.

Not for thy sheaves nor savannas
   Crown we thee, proud Illinois!
Here in his grave is thy grandeur;
   Born of his sorrow thy joy.
Only the tomb by Mount Zion
   Hewn for the Lord do we hold
Dearer than his in thy prairies,
   Girdled with harvests of gold.
Still for the world, through the ages
   Wreathing with glory his brow,
He shall be Liberty's Saviour—
   Freedom's Jerusalem thou!)

By HARRIET M'EWEN KIMBALL.

REST, rest for him whose noble work is done;
   For him who led us gently, unaware,
   Till we were readier to do and dare
For Freedom, and her hundred fields were won.

His march is ended where his march began:
   More sweet his sleep for toil and sacrifice,
   And that rare wisdom whose beginning lies
In fear of God, and charity for man:

And sweetest for the tender faith that grew
   More strong in trial, and through doubt more clear,
   Seeing in clouds and darkness ONE appear
In whose dread name the Nation's sword he drew.

Rest, rest for him; and rest for us to-day
    Whose sorrow shook the land from east to west
    When slain by treason, on the Nation's breast
Her martyr breathed his steadfast soul away.

O fervent heart! O cool and patient head!
    O shoulders broad to bear all others' blame!
    Mercy disguised herself beneath his name,
While Justice through his lips like Pity plead.

His truth could snare the wiliest of the earth;
    His wit outweigh the ponderous debate;
    By sneers unvexed, in triumph unelate,
He stood our chief in place, our chief in worth.

Behold, O kingdoms of the world, behold,
    O mighty powers beyond the swelling wave,
    How fast as rain on his untitled grave
The tears of millions mingle with the mould!

Such love a prince might crave, such homage seek;
    The people's love that clothed him like a king,
    The grateful trust those hands were swift to bring
Whose broken fetters of deliverance speak.

Four years ago unknown—to-day how dear!
    Four years that tried him with a century's strain,
    While treason led his wretched hosts in vain
And turned assassin when his doom was near.

Four little years whose space a thought may span;
    A niche in Time's vast hall where he doth stand,
    To win applause in every age and land,
"The noblest work of God—an HONEST MAN."

DIES IRÆ.

ANONYMOUS.

OH! not the man alone, nor yet the chief
He is, whose death hath robed the land in grief;
A myriad murders centre in the deed,
And with one wound a nation's arteries bleed!

The gory stains that streak the dusk of time
Grow faint and pallid in this noon of crime,
And the great record shudders through its leaves
With the vast groan a people's bosom heaves!

From sea to sea an awful murmur flows,
And, as an avalanche, gathers as it goes,
Till, like volcanic thunder to the skies,
From the shaken earth the cries of vengeance rise!

We will have justice! But we may not bring
Him back who was the guardian of our spring,
Who watched and toiled beneath the sombre skies,
Till from the waste he saw new bloom arise.

Patient and pure, one-minded, undismayed;
Of all the wisdom God vouchsafed, he made
A steadfast use, and if his judgment ran
Astray, or halted—he was but a man!

A simple man he was, who felt his way
Bravely through darkness, hoping for the day,

And praying for more light; yet constant still,
To one great purpose with his single will!

God rest him! He hath fallen at his post
As nobly as the noblest in our host
Of martyrs laurel-crowned! And we, bereft,
Look through the gloom, and murmur—"Who is left?"

By CALEB DUNN.

BEAR him toward the setting sun—
    Home to his Mecca in the West:
There, where the mighty rivers run,
    Make him a grave in his country's breast.

Close to the heart of the mourning land,—
    Close to its beating, O lay him down!
Lay him, O nation, with loving hand—
    Lay him, the ruler without a crown!

Not with the pomp of an idle hour,
    Not with the mockery of art,
Not with the empty show of power,—
    But with the pageantry of the heart.

Bear him across the prairies wide,
    Over the mountain's sunny verge,
Over the rivers whose breathing tide
    Chants for the dead its grandest dirge.

'Lay him beside the violet bed,
  Lay him beneath his native sod;
Under the grass with clover red,
  And bright with th' approving smile of God.

Hallow'd the place where you lay him down,
  While numberless ages lapse away,
Marked with the martyr's cross and crown,
  And bright with the dawn of liberty's day.

For, though no marble urn arise
  Above the grave that holds his dust,
And though no pillar pierce the skies,
  Nor 'scutcheon high, nor sculptured bust;

Still, long as the stars shall kiss the sea,
  Long as the rolling earth shall move,
His name his monument shall be
  Reared in the living heart of love.

By EMELINE SHERMAN SMITH.

LOW he lies upon his bier,
  Slain by traitorous hand;
Low he lies, our Ruler dear,
  Mourned thro' all the land.

Not a voice but wails his doom;
  Not an eye but weeps—
Love, in every heart and home,
  Saddest vigil keeps.

He was not of high degree,
   Nor of lofty birth,
Yet no grander man than he
   Ever trod the earth.

Emperor nor crownèd king
   May with him compare;
Emperor nor crownèd king
   May *his* greatness share.

He was noble in his life;
   Nobler in his death,
For he spake the words of love
   With his latest breath.

Traitors, cowards, rebel foes
   Vilified his name,
Yet his generous spirit ne'er
   Breathed reproach or blame.

Trials gloomed around his path
   Till his day was done,
Yet he kept his course through all,
   Changeless as the sun.

Not for friend, and not for foe
   Would he e'er depart
From the promptings, wise and kind,
   Of his own great heart.

Thro' our country's woeful war—
   Thro' Rebellion's Night,

He was steadfast as a star
    To the Truth and Right.

When at last sweet Victory came
    Dawning o'er the land,
What forgiving words he breathed
    To each rebel band!

While the music of these words
    Lingered on his tongue;
While his praises and his fame
    Through the Nation rung!

While we loved and prized him most
    Came the traitor's blow—
In the hour of peace and joy,
    Came to lay him low.

Ah! the pitying hosts of Heaven,
    Who are watching still
O'er the wild misdeeds of earth,
    Saw this mighty ill—

Saw, with tears, the people's friend
    Basely stricken down,
And they crowned him, as he fell,
    With the martyr's crown.

Now, secure his earthly fame!
    Now, he cannot die!
Angels this decree proclaim
    From their thrones on high.

Still his virtues speak, as when
  He had voice and breath;
Still his kindly acts survive
  His most piteous death.

Blameless life and gentle deeds
  Win the noblest fame;
These, with holiest light, have wreathed
  Our dead Martyr's name.

By JOSEPH MERREFIELD.

OH! martyr to thy country's cause,
  Upholder of her outraged laws,
A sorrowing nation weeps and draws
        Around thy bier.

Not even in thy hour of might,
When in that holiest cause—the right—
Thy armies put their foes to flight,
        Wert thou so dear.

Nor when thy pen, with power unspoken,
Proclaimed the bondsmen's shackles broken,
And gave thy signature, in token,
        A deathless fame,

Wert thou as loved, as prized as now,
When death's pale chaplet wreathes thy brow,
And but remains the patriot's vow,
        Who breathes thy name.

Oh! mothers, teach each infant's tongue
The name of him whose race is run,
Once Freedom's—now Fame's—favorite son,
    Though in the tomb.

Oh! banner of the azure field,
Of silvered stars and shing shield,
Craped be thy folds, that never yield
    To show our gloom.

From the LONDON PUNCH.

YOU lay a wreath on murdered Lincoln's bier!
  You, who with mocking pencil wont to trace,
Broad for the self-complacent British sneer,
  His length of shambling limb, his furrowed face,

His gaunt, gnarled hands, his unkempt, bristling hair,
  His garb uncouth, his bearing ill at ease,
His lack of all we prize as debonair,
  Of power or will to shine, of art to please!

You, whose smart pen backed up the pencil's laugh,
  Judging each step, as though the way were plain;
Reckless, so it could point its paragraph
  Of chief's perplexity, or people's pain!

Beside this corpse, that bears for winding-sheet
  The stars and stripes he lived to rear anew,
Between the mourners at his head and feet,
  Say, scurril-jester, is there room for *you*?

Yes, he had lived to shame me from my sneer—
  To lame my pencil, and confute my pen—
To make me own this hind of princes peer,
  This rail-splitter a true-born king of men.

My shallow judgment I had learnt to rue,
  Noting how to occasion's height he rose;
How his quaint wit made home-truth seem more true;
  How, iron-like, his temper grew by blows;

How humble, yet how hopeful, he could be;
  How in good fortune and in ill the same;
Nor bitter in success, nor boastful he,
  Thirsty for gold, nor feverish for fame.

He went about his work—such work as few
  Ever had laid on head, and heart, and hand—
As one who knows where there's a task to do;
  Man's honest will must Heaven's good grace command;

Who trusts the strength will with the burden grow,
  That God makes instruments to work his will,
If but that will we can arrive to know,
  Nor tamper with the weights of good and ill.

So he went forth to battle, on the side
  That he felt clear was Liberty's and Right's,
As in his peasant boyhood he had plied
  His warfare with rude nature's thwarting mights;—

The uncleared forest, the unbroken soil,
  The iron bark that turns the lumberer's axe,

The rapid, that o'erbears the boatman's toil,
   The prairie, hiding the mazed wanderer's tracks,

The ambushed Indian, and the prowling bear—
   Such were the needs that helped his youth to train:
Rough culture—but such trees large fruit may bear,
   If but their stocks be of right girth and grain.

So he grew up, a destined work to do,
   And lived to do it: four long-suffering years'
Ill-fate, ill-feeling, ill-report, lived through,
   And then he heard the hisses change to cheers,

The taunts to tribute, the abuse to praise,
   And took both with the same unwavering mood;
Till, as he came on light, from darkling days,
   And seemed to touch the goal from where he stood,

A felon hand, between the goal and him,
   Reached from behind his back, a trigger prest—
And those perplexed and patient eyes were dim,
   Those gaunt, long-laboring limbs were laid to rest!

The words of mercy were upon his lips,
   Forgiveness in his heart and on his pen,
When this vile murderer brought swift eclipse
   To thoughts of peace on earth, good-will to men.

The old world and the new, from sea to sea,
   Utter one voice of sympathy and shame!
Sore heart, so stopped when it at last beat high;
   Sad life, cut short just as its triumph came.

A deed accurst! Strokes have been struck before
  By the assassin's hand, whereof men doubt
If more of horror or disgrace they bore;
  But thy foul crime, like Cain's, stands darkly out.

Vile hand, that brandest murder on a strife,
  Whate'er its grounds, stoutly and nobly striven;
And with the martyr's crown crownest a life,
  With much to praise, little to be forgiven!

By ALICE CARY.
Inscribed to the London Punch.

NO glittering chaplet brought from other lands!
  As in his life, this man, in death, is ours;
His own loved prairies o'er his "gaunt gnarled hands,"
  Have fitly drawn their sheet of summer flowers!

What need hath he now of a tardy crown,
  His name from mocking jest and sneer to save?
When every ploughman turns his furrow down
  As soft as though it fell upon his grave.

He was a man whose like the world again
  Shall never see, to vex with blame or praise;
The landmarks that attest his bright, brief reign,
  Are battles, not the pomps of gala-days!

The grandest leader of the grandest war
  That ever time in history gave a place;

What were the tinsel flattery of a star
   To such a breast! or what a ribbon's grace!

'Tis to th' man, and th' man's honest worth,
   The nation's loyalty in tears upsprings;
Through him the soil of labor shines henceforth
   High o'er the silken broideries of kings.

The mechanism of external forms—
   The shrifts that courtiers put their bodies through,
Were alien ways to him—his brawny arms
   Had other work than posturing to do!

Born of the people, well he knew to grasp
   The wants and wishes of the weak and small;
Therefore we hold him with no shadowy clasp—
   Therefore his name is household to us all.

Therefore we love him with a love apart
   From any fawning love of pedigree—
His was the royal soul and mind and heart—
   Not the poor outward shows of royalty.

Forgive us, then, O friends, if we are slow
   To meet your recognition of his worth—
We're jealous of the very tears that flow
   From eyes that never loved a humble hearth.

ANONYMOUS.

BEAR him to his Western home,
  Whence he came four years ago;
Not beneath some mighty dome,
But where Freedom's airs may come,
  Where the prairie grasses grow,
  To the friends who loved him so.

Take him to his quiet rest;
  Toll the bell and fire the gun;
He who served his country best,
He whom millions loved and blest,
  Now has fame immortal won;
  Rack of brain and heart is done.

Shed thy tears, O April rain,
  O'er the bed wherein he sleeps!
Wash away the bloody stain!
Drape the skies in grief, O rain!
  Lo! a nation with thee weeps,
Grieving o'er her martyred slain.

To the people whence he came,
  Bear him gently back again.
Greater his than victor's fame;
His is now a sainted name;
  Never king had such a reign—
  Never people had such pain.

By GEORGE W. RAENHART.

THOUGHTFULLY, watchfully,
  Bend o'er the dead,
Close the eyes carefully,
  Pillow the head.

Gentle ones decently
  Those pale hands fold,
Pulseless, so rigidly
  Stiffened and cold.

Noiselessly, breathlessly,
  Cover the breast,
Bear him then tenderly
  Home to the West.

Wistfully, anxiously,
  Garland the brow,
Silently, solemnly,
  Reverently bow.

Lovingly, tenderly,
  Lay him to rest,
Sorrowing mournfully
  Over the blest.

Twine for him lastingly
  Chaplet and wreath,
Fame shall enduringly
  Honor bequeath.

Guide us, O, Providence,
  Through this red sea,
By thy omnipotence
  Lead us to thee.

Placidly, soothingly,
  Soften our grief,
Father, O, patiently
  Give us relief.

Sighing still heavily,
  O'er the loved slain,
Weeping yet bitterly,
  Groaning with pain.

Tremblingly, dirgefully,
  Accents of woe
From our lips, wearily,
  Ceaselessly flow.

Lord, for thy merciful
  Kindness and care,
Look we still trustingly
  Upward in pray'r.

Leaning confidingly,
  Father, on thee,
Plead we, deliver us
  From out the red sea.

By J. G. BARNETT.

WEEP, oh! weep! A nation weeps;
Weep, oh! weep with tears of anguish;
For the ruler of our land—
Our country's guard, our country's guide—
The nation's hope, the nation's pride—
Has passed away, to dwell with God
In endless day!
Weep, oh! weep! a nation mourns.

All the hopes in him we've cherished,
Are blighted and forever gone!
Tears now speak the nation's feeling;
Bitter tears our grief revealing,
For him who was our pride and stay,
Has passed away to dwell with God
In endless day.
Weep, &c.

Lord of life, to Thee we bend;
Let Thy Spirit now descend;
To the nation whisper peace;
Bid its streams of sorrow cease;
When the summons calls us home,
May we at Thy right hand be found,
With him for whom we grieve and mourn,
So sad and sudden from us torn!
Weep, &c.

By A. J. H. DUGANNE.

O! WEEP for freedom's martyr! Weep! ye nations!
His cause was yours, and yours his aspirations!
Weep! freedmen! weep! redeemed from chains and
    lashes:
Weep! traitors! weep! beneath rebellion's ashes!

He was your friend! His large, warm heart was yielded
Even to his foes. His love their hatred shielded.
Clothed with our wrath, and trampling treason's curses,
Smiles were his lightnings and his bolts were mercies.

Foremost of men—and worthiest of all victors—
States were his rods, and patriot-chiefs his lictors!
Laureled with love, and crowned with thorns of suf-
    fering,
Victim and priest—he dies—our last peace-offering!

This is Good Friday!—day of expiation!
Day of all days, which gave the world salvation
When, by our Lord and Saviour's crucifixion,
Manhood was lifted—unto resurrection!

Day of remembrance! shrined in freedom's story!
Dark with her grief, yet lustrous with her glory!
Day when her stars from Sumter's shield were riven!
Day when her chief surmounts the stars of heaven!

Under his glorious feet our war-cloud drifteth:
Borne on his breast, a ransomed race he lifteth;

Heroes and saints with fadeless stars have crowned him—
And Washington's dear arms are clasped around him!

God of our land! to Thee this pure oblation!
Freedom's sweet blood, poured out for freedom's nation!
Deign to behold our cross and crucifixion,
And be his martyrdom our resurrection!

By J. HENRY HAYWARD.

IF ever man had cause to weep,
  Ay, weep as man, strong man, alone can weep,
That cause is now! Now may he bow his head,
And shade with trembling hand his burning eyes,
Whilst down his cheek the scalding drops of grief
May course their way unchecked, and unreproved
By those whose brows serene with shame would glow,
To own the presence of a single tear,
If shed for cause less grievous and sad
Than this, o'er which a bow'd down nation now
Shames not to weep!

  There is a time when tears
Belong to other than a maiden's eyes—
When man, bold in the consciousness of might,
May without shame forget his stern manhood,
And like a very child bend down and weep—
Weep for a people's happiness destroyed.
Weep for the dream of promised greatness gone,
Weep for sweet peace departed with the day,

Which, mid the gloom of night, went out,
When hell had found a fiend so recreant
Among the sons of earth, as he, whose hands
Hath the pure altar of fraternal right
Besmeared with blood, and draped with sable folds
Each fireside throughout the land!

  My country, oh! I weep for thee.
Beside the ruins of his fallen clay
I weep; nor shame I at the tears thus shed,
For now each sigh is but a bitter oath,
Each tear a seal, which makes the oath a bond,
That every loyal heart doth feel, and swear
Upon the altar of his country's cause—
Which, by the sacrilegious hand of one
Who would deface the noblest work of God
Without a sigh—hath been outraged,
As never did a fiend the laws of God
Or man outrage before!

  A thrill of horror through the nation sweeps,
And tears of anguish from the eyelash fall;
All party ties and lines forgotten are;
And thus in grief—if not in patriotic joy—
The nation is as one!

  'Twere well to weep such tears.
They purge the heart, and to the soul give strength
To do great deeds, when deeds are needed most.
Who loves his country therefore shame not now
O'er her great woe, with me, to weep!

By CHARLES G. HALPINE.

HE filled the nation's eye and heart,
    An honored, loved, familiar name;
  So much a brother, that his fame
Seemed of our lives a common part.

His towering figure, sharp and spare,
    Was with such nervous tension strung,
    As if on each strained sinew swung
The burden of a people's care.

His changing face what pen can draw—
    Pathetic, kindly, droll, or stern?
    And with a glance so quick to learn
The inmost truth of all he saw.

Pride found no idle space to spawn
    Her fancies in his busy mind;
    His worth—like health of air—could find
No just appraisal till withdrawn.

He was his country's—not his own!
    He had no wish but for her weal;
    Nor for himself could think or feel
But as a laborer for her throne.

Her flag upon the heights of power,
    Stainless and unassailed to place—
    To this one end his earnest face
Was bent through every burdened hour.

* * *

The veil that hides from our dull eyes
  A hero's worth, Death only lifts;
  While he is with us, all his gifts
Find hosts to question, few to prize.

But done the battle—won the strife,
  When torches light his vaulted tomb,
  Broad gems flash out and crowns illume
The clay cold brows undecked in life.

And men of whom the world will talk
  For ages hence, may noteless move;
  And only, as they quit us, prove
That giant souls have shared our walk;

For Heaven—aware what follies lurk
  In our weak hearts—their mission done,
  Snatches her loved ones from the sun
In the same hour that crowns their work.

* * *

Oh, loved and lost! thy patient toil
  Had robed our cause in Victory's light;
  Our country stood, redeemed and bright,
With not a slave on all her soil.

Again o'er Southern towns and towers
  The eagles of our nation flew;
  And as the weeks to summer grew
Each day a new success was ours.

'Mid peal of bells and cannon-bark,
  And shouting streets with flags abloom,
  Sped the shrill arrow of thy doom,
And in an instant all was dark!

    *   *   *

Thick clouds around us seem to press;
  The heart throbs quickly—then is still;
  Father, 'tis hard to say, "Thy will
Be done!" in such an hour as this.

A martyr to the cause of man,
  His blood is freedom's eucharist,
  And in the world's great hero list
His name shall lead the van!

Yea! raised on faith's white wings, unfurled
  In heaven's pure light, of him we say:
  "He fell on the self-same day
A GREATER DIED TO SAVE THE WORLD."

By Rev. EDWARD HOPPER.

REBELLION! thou hast done thy worst;
  O treason-spawn of slavery!
Thy work is done. Now take thy crown—
  The felon-cap of infamy.

Thou foulest murderer since Cain,
  Whose heart like his gave murder birth,
Go thou, accursed of God and man,
  A vagabond upon the earth.

This crimsonest, bloodiest-red of all
   The blossoms and the fruit of crime,
Shall make man blush that he is man,
   Through all the coming years of time

A nation's songs, of joyous praise,
   Rising to God on every gale,
Were in a moment hushed into
   A nation's broken-hearted wail.

A nation's hands while weaving flowers,
   To place upon her ruler's brow,
Were palsied by thy murder-blow,
   And hang in sullen sorrow now.

The piteous night that saw the deed,
   From all her starry eyes did weep;
And earth grew restless with such blood,
   And blushed while yet it lay asleep.

The day arose, but shrunk aghast,
   And wrapped a cloud around the sun,
To hide his face from that foul crime,
   And wept great tears, as night had done.

O treason-spawn of slavery!
   Snake, warmed within a nation's breast,
How couldst thou crawl, unseen, so high,
   And strike our eagle in his nest?

Once seeming angel—devil now,
   Damned with eternal stain of blood,

Thy name is cursed, like Lucifer's,
  That rebel who first struck at God.

Thy victim's blood hath stained thy brow,
  As thou didst scar thy bondmen's skin;
And the fierce lightnings of God's wrath
  Shall scorch, and sear, and burn it in.

Thou'st saved what thou didst mean to kill,
  O rage most foul and impotent!
For freedom hath her martyr crowned,
  And we our martyr-President!

A martyr's crown is on his head,
  The cap of infamy on thine;
Thou liv'st to die a felon-death,
  He died to live a life divine.

For him eternal glory shines,
  An endless fame throughout all time;
But what for thee but blood-red flame
  Of endless death for blood-red crime?

What peerless blood once filled his heart,
  And thousands', shed for liberty!
O treason! look upon thy hands;
  'Tis all on thee, 'tis all on thee!

Assassin of a President!
  Thou hast not killed our native land,
But thou hast murdered tender love,
  And sealed thy doom with bloody hand.

Sweet angel Mercy smiled by him,
   While sitting on the people's throne;
But thou hast slain the angel there,
   And left stern Nemesis alone.

The lightning stroke that broke our hearts
   Hath melted all our hearts in one,
And drank up all our pitying tears;
   O sulphurous flame, what hast thou done?

Our iron wills are melted now,
   All, all in one stern, iron sword;
And from that sword the martyr-blood
   Cries out for vengeance to the Lord.

Wail, wail, O North! wail, wail, O South!
   Mercy is dead, but justice lives;
And law rides forth with Penalty:
   For that sweet tongue no more forgives.

That shattered brain so toiled for thee!
   That murdered heart did love thee so!
Wail, wail, O South! thou treason-cursed,
   Poor words cannot express thy woe.

Since Washington, no man hath sat,
   (Unconscious greatness all his own,)
So good, so great, so grandly wise,
   So meekly on the people's throne.

Like Washington, he lived to save
   A race from thraldom, and he died

As loved, revered, and wept as he,
  To stand in glory by his side.

Repenting tongues, in sorrow clad,
  Come gathering round his body slain,
To pluck, alas! their arrows thence
  Which stung his living heart with pain.

Eyes weep in love for him, to whom,
  Alive, no loving look they gave;
And foemen's hands cast evergreen,
  And sweet, white flowers into his grave.

A nation's eyes are blind with grief;
  A nation's heart is drowned in grief;
Kingdoms and crowns join in our grief;
  Mankind is sobbing with our grief.

And never yet for man hath grief
  From broken hearts so wept and cried,
Like that long moan from weeping slaves,
  The lowly ones for whom he died.

Their hearts are broken with their chains;
  Their Moses, who did lead them through
The wilderness to Canaan's shore,
  From Pisgah caught the pleasant view;

Then in a moment heard the voice
  Of him who set the captives free
And claims the glory, say to him,
  "Friend, come up higher; sit with me!"

Could we solidify the tears
   Shed for the martyr-President,
Those precious jewels were enough,
   Piled up, to build his monument!

By HENRY MORFORD.

TO every man—Horatius said—
   Death cometh soon or falleth late!
But only he the blow should dread
   Who begs, not dares, his fate.

To every man some post is given
   Where honors point or duties call;
And if his doom is writ of heaven,
   'Tis there that he should fall.

No matter if the battle shout
   Drowns the last lingering sob of breath,
Or woman's feeble wail moans out
   Round some hushed bed of death.

No matter if the strong hand hold,
   That moment, grasp of duty's helm,
Or if soft joys the limbs enfold,
   Or midnight slumber whelm.

No matter—so the path is clear.
   No matter—so the will is strong,
No matter if the doom is near,
   Or waits and tarries long.

To die in God's good time is gain,
    Whether he takes, in loving peace,—
Or murderous stroke of hand and brain
    Makes quick and sad surcease.

But oh! to die with labor done—
    That labor what the whole world willed,
Or with the goal so nearly won,
    All hold the task fulfilled,—

To have gained a victor's glorious wreath,
    Then crowned it with the sapphire star
Of a great mercy's trust and faith,
    Brightening the worlds afar,—

To know the midnight gone at last,
    To see the day break clear and calm,
To know that o'er the black vales past
    The morning breathes its balm,—

To stand upon the mountain's top,
    Such toil just closed, at such an hour,
And cloudward, whence God's blessings drop,
    Hear man's sweep up with power,—

And then and there to die! To rest!
    Marbled in fame—embalmed in good!
The past (once doubted) praised and blest,
    The future understood,–

No heat and burden of to-day
    Stretching its vista on before—

The immortal seizing mortal clay,
    As Moses once they bore—

Death at the summit, this! Not death—
    A happy apotheosis
That men might seek with praying breath
    A thousand years, and miss!

And when ye hunt his murderers down—
    Men who his mantle humbly bear—
And blast them with a nation's frown,
    And limb from carcase tear—

Do it, because the nation's pride
    And God's quick justice this demand—
That never more the regicide
    May lift his reeking hand;

But do it not in hot revenge
    For one, unsuffering by the blow,
Who at the summit found a change
    That only God can know.

And when ye shroud your halls in gloom,
    And raise the prayer, and drop the tear,
And bear him to his western tomb,
    A nation round his bier—

Weep for the country, if ye must—
    For manhood, murder-stained and dim;
But dwarf not judgment, truth and trust,
    By shedding tears for him!

A CRIME WITHOUT A NAME.

By EUGENE H. MUNDAY.

LONG years of teaching yield a fruit
   That well the demon's brow may shame;
And nations stand aghast and mute
   Before a crime without a name!

So firmly good, so kindly brave,
   He knit our hearts unto his own;
And, bowing o'er our martyr's grave,
   We pray—God keep him near his throne!

But who shall stand before the power
   That's gathering from the nation's grief,
While, stricken low in triumph's hour,
   We mourn our loved, our father chief?

How will our heroes bear the blow?
   Or how restrain their bursting wrath?
As onward to the Gulf they go,
   Will fiery besoms sweep their path?

O, guide our vengeance! Thou to whom
   The power of wrath alone belongs!
Let not blind nature, in the gloom,
   With sickening carnage right our wrongs;

But while pale Mercy bleeding lies,
   Dumb, on her dear apostle's grave,

Let Justice, with her piercing eyes
   And nerveful arm, advance—to save!

To save the weak, the driven foe,
   Yet smite, as with Thy sword of flame,
The fiends—o'ermatching fiends below—
   Who taught a crime without a name!

By OLIVER WENDELL HOLMES.

O THOU of soul and sense and breath,
   The ever-present Giver,
Unto Thy mighty angel, death,
   All flesh thou dost deliver;
What most we cherish, we resign,
For life and death alike are Thine,
   Who reignest Lord forever!

Our hearts lie buried in the dust
   With him, so true and tender,
The patriot's stay, the people's trust,
   The shield of the offender;
Yet every murmuring voice is still,
As, bowing to Thy sovereign will,
   Our best loved we surrender.

Dear Lord, with pitying eye behold
   This martyr generation,
Which Thou, through trials manifold,
   Art showing Thy salvation!

O let the blood by murder spilt
Wash out Thy stricken children's guilt,
   And sanctify our nation!

Be Thou Thy orphaned Israel's friend,
   Forsake Thy people never,
In One our broken Many blend,
   That none again may sever!
Hear us, O Father, while we raise
With trembling lips our song of praise,
   And bless Thy name forever!

By MRS. LUCY HAMILTON HOOPER.

> "Lass rinnen der Thränen
> Vergeblichen Lauf!
> Es wecke die Klage
> Den Todten nicht auf!"
>   SCHILLER. *Thekla's Song.*

> "Stream forth, O tears!
> Ye pour in vain;
> No plaints awaken
> The dead again."
>   *Translation.*

AMID the grief of this awful time,
   Shadowed by sorrow and dark with crime,
Our hearts are haunted by Schiller's rhyme,
   "Lass rinnen die Thränen."

O wondrous vision of Wallenstein!
The days of treason and triumph shine,
A sad voice murmurs the boding line,
   "Lass rinnen die Thränen."

The laugh and the shout ring from the walls,
There's mirth and feasting amid the halls,
The mournful song to the echo calls,
   " Lass rinnen die Thränen."

We were so joyous a while ago,
Our hearts and our homes were all aglow,
No Thekla beside us whispered low,
   " Lass rinnen die Thränen."

Brightly dawned our victorious day,
Proudly we greeted its noontide ray,
Its sun in darkness has passed away,
   " Lass rinnen die Thränen."

Our cannon's thunder seemed faint and low
To utter our joy; but now, ah now!
We whisper sadly, we whisper low,
   " Lass rinnen die Thränen."

Our lips were smiling, our hearts were gay,
The noblest heart in the land is clay,
And now though *his* smile fadeth not away,
   " *Lass rinnen die Thränen.*"

By W. H. C. HOSMER.

THE muffled drum and tolling bell
    Betoken ill the nation's grief,
While bearing to his narrow cell
    All that is mortal of their chief.

Such heart-felt homage to the great
    And laureled Julius was not paid,
When lay the pleading corse in state,
    Yet unavenged his mighty shade.

Let childhood drop the wreaths of May,
    Fair women place choice funeral flowers
Above his grandly-coffined clay—
    The palm is his, the cross is ours.

In mourning is Columbia clad,
    In black her starry banner veiled,
And bosoms, late with triumph glad,
    Throb now for final conflict mailed.

When humbled was the flag in dust
    Whose stars blaze over Sumter now,
His arm, in God reposing trust,
    He lifted, smiting treason's brow.

Avengers, full of prowess, woke
    To hear his clarion call, "to arms!"
Forsaking, for the roar and smoke
    Of battle-fields, their shops and farms.

From frowning North, and loyal East,
  Our young West with its broad domain
Rise wailing for the great high priest
  Of mercy, truth and justice slain.

His mission is not ended here,
  Nor is his sun of glory set;
To all in bonds his words of cheer
  Give promise of deliverance yet.

Guilt only struck the mortal down,
  The deathless, murder could not kill;
Earth's martyrs who have won the crown
  Die never, guiding, guardian still.

ANONYMOUS.

GIVE place to sorrow; fill the heavy air
  With wailing, and sad sounding requiem,
While bell slow tolling, and deep muffled drum,
Mingle their echoes in a funeral hymn.
Grief, pallid phantom, spread thy letheal wing
Above us! Horror, wild-eyed, distraught, draw near!
And murkest night, your darkest shadows fling;—
The patriot! Martyr! rests upon his bier;—
Then high the requiem swell; while falls the silent tear!

Chief of a mighty nation thou art gone,
Sudden and swift as tempest to their mark,
No more to buffet blasting storms of state,
Thy soul has found a refuge in the Ark

Of mercy—so we trust, no more can dark
And hellish hate assail thee; never more—
Thy glorious course is run! Thy stranded bark
Has reached the port of peace; thro' seas of gore,
Through scorching fires of hell; thank God they all
    are o'er!

Droop low, blue banner, wreath thy starry folds
Above his silent clay, his pulseless head,
The flag he loved shall guard his slumbers well;
Till dust to dust, he mingles with the dead.
What precious dust! all hallow'd be the bed
Where Lincoln sleeps—shrined in a nation's heart
Forever—at thy name the helpless who have bled
Beneath the pang of power, shall sudden start
Into new life, and bless the sound while glows the
    vital spark.

Conqu'ring Columbia comes from well-fought fields
To lay her trophies at her chieftain's feet,
What tho' he sleeps among the lowly dead?
His soul from starry-ether still shall greet
His brothers, children, friends, Oh! it is meet
To name him reverently, and with pride—
Tell how the deadly fire of traitors beat
On his devoted head! tell far and wide,
How wisely, nobly, Lincoln lived! how like a martyr
    died!

Saint John, New Brunswick.

MEMORY OF ABRAHAM LINCOLN.

BY J. A. FIELD.

THANK God, that he was caught at last!
   Thank God, that he is dead!
That tribulation has laid low
   The dark assassin's head.
Oh, modern Judas! traitor—knave!
   Whose base blood-thirsty soul
Was dyed within the blackened streams,
   That downward, death-ward roll.

Greater than Cain's, that heinous crime
   Committed by his hand,
Against our Nation's mighty Chief,
   The Father of our land.
"Grandfather," said a little maid,
   Standing beside his knee,
"What is a dark assassin?—please
   Explain it all to me."

"Darling, it is a vile, bad man,
   That like a panther creeps
From out some covert's hidden depths,
   And on his victim leaps.
No trembling of his iron nerves,
   No pity in his breast,
While sending prayerless and unshriven,
   A brother to his rest."

"Oh good, kind Lincoln!—it was mean—
    Had not the assassin shame?
Grandfather, tell me, if you please,
    What was the murderer's name?"
"My love, 'twould soil a loyal lip,
    'Tis stained so by his crime;
Traitor will be its synonym,
    Throughout all coming time."

"And where, pray, will his body lie?
    Where his deep-sunken grave?
Sure, 'twill not with the soldiers rest,
    Our noble and our brave?"
"No, love, his grave will never meet
    Man's wonder-loving eyes;
No tell-tale marble ever show
    Where the vile traitor lies.

"Unknown, unwept, unhonored, too,
    Resolves the senseless clay;
None, none can seek the secret spot,
    For none can point the way.
Earth claims her part of crumbling dust,
    And so the water, air;
But the immortal—oh, my God!
    Where is the spirit—where?"

New Orleans.

TO MRS. LINCOLN.

By EMISSUS.

OH! gracious God, do lend thine ear,
   In tender love and zeal,
To this heart-rending, humble prayer,
   And this sincere appeal,
For her whose heart is bow'd in grief,
   For him she loved so dear—
Who finds nor comfort nor relief,
   Tho' constant tears appear.

Lord, give her strength to cast aside,
   This mournful wail of mind,
With trusting heart let her confide,
   That she may surely find
Comfort from those who love her true,
   With constancy replete,
From faithful breasts where friendship grew
   And blooms so pure and sweet.

Severe affliction has been thrown
   Upon her earthly peace;
While sorrow's web has quickly grown
   To bind without release:
Her life's upon a stormy sea,
   Tossed by a gloomy gale,
Along the shores where troubles flee
   Deep in a dolesome vale.

Father, her mind with rapture lift
   To Christian's brightest scope
Of heavenly joy—this precious gift
   Will give her strength to hope
That all her trials shall allay
   Into a peaceful form
Of happiness, to drive away
   Affliction's darkest storm.

And tho' her heart be fully clothed
   With Mary's sinful grief,
More sinful yet, may be betrothed
   With murmurings for relief,
Yet give her strength to purge the sin
   By pure and contrite heart,
Till truly cleansed, without, within,
   And all her sins depart.

The floating clouds around, portray
   Such dark and dismal hues:
Oh! Lord, disperse this sad array,
   Into refreshing dews,
To spread the path with righteous grace,
   With holy light of love;
Which sacred gift let her embrace,
   'Twill all her grief remove.

The cares intrusted to her guide,
   Her dearest comfort be;
Whose years, I pray, may gently glide
   In peace o'er life's sad sea.

While blooming in capacious mind
  In wisdom's fertile grove,
May gather thence the wisest kind
  Of knowledge from above.

Then let the brightest pleasures roll
  Across her peaceful breast,
Until the solemn knell shall toll
  Her breath to silent rest.
Then may her soul but realize
  The blessing from above,
Eternal joys—the only prize
  Of God's redeeming love.

As twilight hours doth softly link
  Day's beauties with the night;
And as the morning beams shall drink
  The darkness from the light:
So may death as gently fling
  His mantle o'er her eyes,
While angels, with protecting wings,
  Shall waft her to the skies.

Charleston, S. C.

By ALBERT LAIGHTON.

TOLL, oh death-bells, sad and slow;
  Muffled drums, your dirges play;
Freedom's martyr lieth low,—
  And a nation weeps to-day.

Silent be the busy mart;
   Midway droop, oh flags, in air,
While the country's bleeding heart
   Sobs its bitter grief in prayer.

God of nations, as our tears
   In this hour of darkness flow,—
Hush our murmurings, calm our fears;
   Lift the crushing weight of woe.

Let us feel Thine arms beneath,
   Oh, thou Holy One and Just;
Teach our trembling lips to breathe,
   "In the Lord we put our trust."

By E. B. P——.

IN silent honor side by side,
   Amazed the New and Old Worlds stand,
   Since by the foul assassin's hand
Lincoln, the pure and true, hath died.

We cannot speak the thing we meant—
   Excess of grief hath made us dumb,
   (Few words from stricken spirits come),
Only our tears are eloquent.

Great ruler of a mighty land!
   A *king* in deed though not in name,
   Thy sense of right the only fame
Sought by the life so calm and grand.

Rest—for thy work is done. Thy hand
  Hath written freedom for the slave;—
  His chains are buried in thy grave;
His curse is lifted from the land.

The fame thou didst not seek is thine:
  Both life and death have stricken hands
  To make thee famous in all lands,
And the great human heart thy shrine.
Brighton, England.

By ETA.

OUT of the depths, O Lord! out of the depths
  A smitten nation cries to Thee—
  Bowed by the awful mystery
Of death; sitting with sackcloth thickly spread,
Mourning, uncomforted, its honored dead.
  Alas! alas! we're weak to-day;
  A prince has gone! our country's stay,
  Its chosen chief, loved of the land,
  Falls in his might by murderous hand!
O God! for such unknown, unfathomed grief,
Thou, only Thou, canst bring us sure relief.

  The nation's heart so late with victory clad,
  Lies bleeding 'neath a ponderous cross,
  Crushed, broken by its mighty loss.
O Lord, our strength, to Thee we turn! for though
Satanic hatred aimed the fatal blow,

>   Thy wisdom didst permit the deed;
>   In its Thy sovereign will we read.
>   Thou hast afflicted! Thou canst heal;
>   Thou sendest grief, Thy love reveal.
> O! calm our spirits, quench the revengeful thought,
> We would be still and trust Thee as we ought.

> Man dies, the highest—but the Eternal lives.
>   Thou Chief Supreme, our Ruler, still
>   Our destiny will hold, fulfil.
> Though treason's factions 'gainst us madly rage,
> Thou canst their wrath restrain, our grief assuage.
>   Thus far, no farther can they go.
>   In Thee, O let this nation trust;
>   And now, from martyred mercy's dust,
> Rise to a loftier faith, a courage strong,
> To battle firmly 'gainst our country's wrong.

> Nerve Thou each heart, guide Thou each faltering arm!
>   Without Thee, chaos will prevail;
>   With Thee our cause can never fail.
> God of the Right! O save our stricken land!
> Vengeance is Thine, we leave it in Thy hand.
>   No martyr's blood is shed in vain;
>   May ours wipe out foul treason's stain;
>   And our dear land to peace restore,
>   To know disunion nevermore.
> Grant this, O Lord! and we will meekly bow
> And kiss the rod that smites so sorely now.

By ALBERT S. EVANS.

ONE mournful wail is heard from shore to shore;
  A Nation's heart is stricken to the core;
And Freedom, kneeling, with uncovered head,
Weeps by the altar of our Country's dead.

O God, who suffered this for purpose high!
Teach us like him to live, like him to die,
True to the last to duty and to right,
Trusting to Thee the issue of the fight.

"Good night to thee, hero, good night to thee, sage!
Good night to thy form, but good morn to thy fame;
Pass on with thy visor up, from age unto age:
Not a sentry to challenge thy deeds or thy name."

San Francisco.

By EVA.

GLAD anthems filled the air,
  Mingled with tears and prayer,
    Through this great land.
"All now seemed well with us,"
  God had defended us,
  His banner over us,
    Held by Love's hand.

From out this bright'ning sky,
When joy and peace seemed nigh,
    Burst forth dread hate!

Our chief, in black laid low!
By the assassin's blow!
Who can guide safely now
    Our Ship of State?

And O! a dark, deep stain
Rests on thine honored name,
    My native land!
With shame thy head is bent,
Thy heart with grief is rent,
By this great judgment, sent
    By God's own hand.

Help us, our fathers' God,
Humbly to kiss Thy rod,
    Though we in pain
Mourn for the noble dead,
Who hath for freedom bled,—
Let not his blood be shed,
    Great God, in vain.

Laurel and myrtle now
Crown his immortal brow,
    On that blest shore.
There, from all toil and pain,
Rests now his weary brain,
Our loss will be his gain,
    Blessed evermore.

MEMORY OF ABRAHAM LINCOLN.

By IOLA.

A PALL of deep darkness is spread o'er the land,
While shadows, grim shadows, like sentinels stand:
A storm of wild fury has burst on our head,
And silent we sit, 'mid the shades of the dead.

The mighty has fallen! the noble, the brave,
The hero God gave us the country to save:
Struck down in a moment by one fatal blow,
Has left us surrounded by trappings of woe.

Ah! never before was our country, I ween,
Of a deed of such horror and blackness the scene;
E'en the stars on our banner grew suddenly pale,
As the telegraph flashed out the strange, fearful tale.

A nation of mourners! a nation in tears,
For the leader lay low in the bloom of his years!
Ay! weep, O Columbia! weep, weep o'er the slain,
For the like of the fallen we'll ne'er see again.

He's gone! our loved father! no breath on his name,
To sully his glory, or tarnish his fame;
His deeds are immortal, his record as bright
As the beams of the morn, or the sun's brilliant light.

He went, ere the fire of his eye had grown dim,
His cup full of honor! ay! full to the brim!
He went when the love of the noble and brave,
Seemed armor sufficient to shield and to save.

He went with the blessings of millions he'd freed
From the tyrant's strong grasp, in the hour of their need;
"God bless Abraham Lincoln!" this, this was the cry,
The prayer that from thousands ascended on high.

He went! our brave Eagle! he soared to the sun!
The warfare accomplished, the victory won!
O, weep not for him! but ah! our loved land—
How can she spare now that firm guiding hand.

* * * * * * *

Ah! cravens! base cravens! that struck the foul blow,
That has draped the whole land in the symbols of woe;
Laugh! laugh at your work! rejoice at the deed,
But know that of justice, you'll reap the full meed.

"Escape!" no escape! there's a God in the sky,
Whose throne of strict justice stands firmly on high,
He's already placed Cain's mark on your brow,
'Twill burn there forever, 'tis burning there now.

"Tyrannis!" "tyrannis!" 'tis false as the soul,
O'er which the dark billows shall fearfully roll!
"*Sic semper tyrannis,*" it's brought you your doom!
E'en now lowers o'er you, the shade of the tomb.

* * * * * * *

Rest, rest thee, loved chieftain! for thee rest is meet!
After labor and turmoil, such rest must be sweet:
Thou has gone to the land where foul treason is not,
Thou hast gone where no traitors disturb thy blest lot.

Pass on with your leader! bear, bear him away!
The tears of a nation are falling to-day:
Tread softly, tread softly, your feet on his sod,
And leave him, the hero, to glory and God.

ANONYMOUS.

THANK God they chose this sacred day
   To seal the covenant with blood,
We might not else His wond'rous way,
   Through waters deep, have understood.

They said of old that "this was He
   Who Israel should redeem, we thought;"
Nor saw in death the mighty key
   To all a Saviour's life had wrought.

Man's wrath but praised his Maker's power,
   And worked the will it would defy.
"Oh fools and slow of heart," this hour,
   Who do not see deliverance nigh!

The stroke that aimed at Judah's heart
   Shall set a nation fully free;
This death shall do its noble part
   In the great work of liberty.

Oh! Easter, glorious Easter morn,
   I see thee on the world arise;
When mighty nations yet unborn
   Shall lift their pean to the skies!

And thank Thee, Lord, for every drop
  Of patriot blood this day has shed;
And for the trumpet-stirring voice
  That loudest speaks, "He being dead."

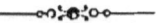

By RICHARD STORRS WILLIS.

NOW wake the requiem's solemn moan,
For him whose patriot task is done!
A nation's heart stands still to-day
With horror, o'er his martyred clay!

O, God of peace, repress the ire,
Which fills our souls with vengeful fire!
Vengeance is Thine,—and sovereign might,
Alone, can such a crime requite!

Farewell, thou good and guileless heart!
The manliest tears for thee must start!
E'en those at times who blamed thee here,
Now deeply sorrow o'er thy bier.

O Jesus, grant him sweet repose,
Who, like Thee, seemed to love his foes!
Those foes, like Thine, their wrath to spend,
Have slain their best, their firmest friend.

(GLORIA.)

Praise God from whom all chast'nings flow!
Praise Him all sorrowing hearts below!
Praise Him above ye martyred host,
Praise Father, Son, and Holy Ghost!

By B. F. TAYLOR.

THERE'S a burden of grief on the breezes of spring,
And a song of regret from the bird on its wing;
There's a pall on the sunshine and over the flowers,
And a shadow of graves on these spirits of ours;
For a star hath gone out from the night of our sky,
On whose brightness we gazed as the war-cloud rolled by;
So tranquil and steady and clear were its beams,
That they fell like a vision of peace on our dreams.

A heart that we knew had been true to our weal,
And a hand that was steadily guiding the wheel;
A name never tarnished by falsehood or wrong,
That had dwelt in our hearts like a soul-stirring song:
Ah! that pure, noble spirit has gone to its rest,
And the true hand lies nerveless and cold on his breast;
But the name and the memory—*these* never will die,
But grow brighter and dearer as ages go by.

Yet the tears of a nation fall over the dead,
Such tears as a nation before never shed,
For our cherished one fell by a dastardly hand,
A martyr to truth and the cause of the land;
And a sorrow has surged like the waves to the shore
When the breath of the tempest is sweeping them o'er;
And the heads of the lofty and lowly have bowed,
As the shaft of the lightning sped out from the cloud.

Not gathered, like Washington, home to his rest,
When the sun of his life was far down in the West;

But strieken from earth in the midst of his years,
With the Canaan in view, of his prayers and his tears.
And the people whose hearts in the wilderness failed,
Sometimes, when the stars of their promise had paled,
Now, stand by his side on the mount of his fame,
And yield him their hearts in a grateful acclaim.

Yet there on the mountain, our Leader must die,
With the fair land of promise spread out to his eye;
His work is accomplished, and what he has done
Will stand as a monument under the sun;
And his name, reaching down through the ages of time,
Will still through the age of eternity shine—
Like a star, sailing on through the depths of the blue,
On whose brightness we gaze every evening anew.

His white tent is pitched on the beautiful plain,
Where the tumult of battle comes never again,
Where the smoke of the war-cloud ne'er darkens the air,
Nor falls on the spirit a shadow of care.
The song of the ransomed enrapture his ear,
And he heeds not the dirges that roll for him here;
In the calm of his spirit, so strange and sublime,
He is lifted far over the discords of time.

Then bear him home gently, great son of the West,
'Mid her fair blooming prairies lay Lincoln to rest;
From the nation who loved him, she takes to her trust,
And will tenderly garner the consecrated dust.
A Mecca his grave to the people shall be,
And a shrine evermore for the hearts of the free.

By GEORGE ADAMS.

SONS of Freedom, bow the head,
Silently and softly tread;
Let no sound of joy arise:
Sorrow dims a nation's eyes.
See, her mighty chief lies low,
See her leader's life-blood flow,
And within her stately halls,
Dark as night the shadow falls.
   Sons of Freedom, bow the head,
   Silently and softly tread.

Chosen by a nation's voice,
Leader of his people's choice,
In his country's darkest hour
See him wield her mighty power,
'Midst her best and bravest stand,
Freely giving heart and hand.
Wise in council, brave in deed,
See him for his children bleed:
   Chosen by a nation's voice,
   Leader of his people's choice.

Not 'mid battle's raging strife
Did the hero yield his life;
Nor with thousands round him lying,
Bleeding, fainting, groaning, dying;
Not while darkening overhead,
Far and near the war-cloud spread,

While a world in wonder gazed,
Awe-struck, breathless and amazed—
  Not 'mid battle's raging strife
  Did the hero yield his life,

But 'mid cheers of victory,
On the day of jubilee,
While triumphant shouts were ringing,
Every voice in gladness singing,
Bright eyes as the starlight gleaming,
Every face with sunshine beaming,
Young and old their praise bestowing,
And each heart with joy o'erflowing
  In the 'midst of victory,
  On the day of jubilee.

Rise, ye brave of every nation,
Rise and brand with execration
Foulest deed and basest plan
E'er conceived by man 'gainst man.
Let your voices to the skies,
Like Niagara's thunder rise,
Breathing curses loud and long
'Gainst the fiends that did the wrong:
  Rise, ye brave of every nation,
  Rise and brand with execration.

Bright around the mighty dead,
See a glorious halo shed:
Hark! a myriad voices rise,
Waft his name beyond the skies,

Mingling their glad songs of praise
With high heaven's angelic lays:
"'Tis," dark Afric's sons have cried,
"For *us* Lincoln lived and died."
    Bright around the mighty dead
    See a glorious halo shed.

Now he, entered into rest,
With earth's noblest, bravest, best,
Hears the Master's words, "Well done,
Good and faithful servant, come,
Enter thou into my joy,
Dwell in bliss without alloy,
Heaven's great joy shall fill thy soul
While eternal ages roll."
    He has entered into rest,
    With earth's noblest, bravest, best.

Belleville, Canada West.

ANONYMOUS.

THE nation groans with one indignant sob,
A great, true heart hath ceased on earth to throb;
Not as in nature's order kindly given,
Sinking in peace to wake again in heaven—
But by a murderer's hand all wildly hurled
Into the mysteries of another world!
Who does not feel that now the deed is done,
How many wronged that noble, virtuous one?
Who does not fear that none can stem the flood
Of vengeance born from that dark deed of blood?

Was there an act of his to wound a heart—
A kindness sought in which he had no part?
Can we remember aught but mindfulness
To pardon, not to punish in distress?
And the light story was it not a wile
From sorrow many a bosom to beguile?
Assassin! he had gone the voyage through,
What could his death avail to such as you?
Safely he guided at the tossing helm,
Through all the storms that threatened to o'erwhelm;
Now he was just to find a sweet release,
An anchor cast upon the shore of Peace.
Illustrious man! so simple yet so great,
The nation is to-day disconsolate,
And until now we feel thou art removed,
We never knew how much thou wert beloved.

New Orleans.

By GEORGE G. W. MORGAN.

HE is gone; he is dead; his pure spirit has fled
    From this earth full of sorrow and woe;
By angels now led to his presence who said:
    "'Tis to gain *you* a welcome I go."

In the realms of the blest his pure soul will find rest,
    Then give way to no more of your sorrow,
'Tis a blessing confessed—the first are the best—
    To make *us* more willing to follow.

MEMORY OF ABRAHAM LINCOLN.

ANONYMOUS.

LOWER the starry flag
   Amid a sovereign people's lamentation
For him the honored ruler of the nation;
   Lower the starry flag!

   Let the great bells be toll'd
Slowly and mournfully in every steeple,
Let them make known the sorrow of the people;
   Let the great bells be toll'd!

   Lower the starry flag,
And let the solemn, sorrowing anthem, pealing,
Sound from the carven choir to fretted ceiling;
   Lower the starry flag!

   Let the great bells be toll'd,
And let the mournful organ music, rolling,
Tune with the bells in every steeple tolling;
   Let the great bells be toll'd!

   Lower the starry flag;
The nation's honored chief in death is sleeping,
And for our loss our eyes are wet with weeping;
   Lower the starry flag!

   Let the great bells be toll'd!
His honest, manly heart has ceased its beating,
His lips no more shall speak the kindly greeting;
   Let the great bells be toll'd!

Lower the starry flag;
No more shall sound his voice in scorn of error,
Filling the traitor's heart with fear and terror;
Lower the starry flag!

Let the great bells be toll'd:
He reverenced the gift which God has given,
Freedom to all, the priceless boon of Heaven,
Let the great bells be toll'd!

Lower the starry flag!
His dearest hopes were wedded with the nation,
He valued more than all the land's salvation;
Lower the starry flag!

Let the great bells be toll'd;
His name shall live on History's brightest pages,
His voice shall sound through Time's remotest ages;
Let the great bells be toll'd!

ANONYMOUS.

BENEATH the vast and vaulted dome
   That copes the Capitol, he lies;
It is a dreary, dreary night;
   The stars in their eternal home
   Seem like the sad ethereal eyes
   Of seraphs, filled with tender light.

The Capitol is wrapped in mist;
Strangely the shadows come and go—
The dome seems floating into air,
   Upborne by unseen hands, I wist—
   In solemn state he lies below,
   His pure hands folded as in prayer.

He lies in solemn state, alone—
Alone with only silence there—
Alone with lofty lamps that rim
   Almost the very coping stone;
   Yet not alone, for all the air
   Is filled with tender thoughts of him.

And all night long the marble floors
Have echoed to the gentle tread
Of blessed and immortal feet;
   And through the open corridors
   The mighty and illustrious dead
   Have thronged all night his face to greet.

And they have bent, full-browed with pain,
And gazed through their celestial tears
Upon the face so dear to them—
   Upon the man whose heart was fain
   Above all hearts these latter years
   To be like his of Bethlehem.

And so our heads are bowed with grief
Because we loved him, and because
But yesterday, this great man stood

Of many states the perfect chief,
Dispensing justice and the laws,
And mindful of the public good.

Alas! it is a dreary night;
For he we loved so much now lies
Beneath the vast and vaulted dome;
And in his eyes there is no light—
No light is in those loving eyes
Which kindliness had made her home.

By OLIVER PERRY MANLOVE.

OUR nation is shrouded in gloom
And sorrow, as never before;
A great man has gone to the shades of the tomb,
That no earthly beacon can ever illume
This side of eternity's shore.

Struck down by a murderer's hand—
A deed that but demons could do—
Urged on and supported by treason's black band,
Filling with mourning our beautiful land,
And draping our Red, White and Blue.

Never more will his voice be heard—
That voice which we loved to hear;
But mem'ry will treasure away every word,
That our hearts in the bygone so deeply has stirr'd,
While we drop the sorrowing tear.

No more on his face will we gaze,
　　Smiling in heaven's soft light;
It never again will be warmed with the rays
Of living fire from the life-blush blaze,
　　To make its loved features bright.

Oh! every pulse is a rest!
　　The burden of life is now o'er;
His spirit has gone from his noble breast,
To dwell in the holy land of the blest,
　　Forever and evermore.

By S. A——.

HUSHED be the voice of mirth—each pean stilled,
　　And let us weep our martyred Chief beside;
While every heart with bitter grief is filled:
　　A noble hero in the cause of truth hath died.

How shall we mourn him?—he who for the right,
　　A firm, undaunted champion was found,
And trusting in the Lord Jehovah's might,
　　Stood, while opposing hosts were gathered round.

How shall we mourn him?—how pay the tribute due,
　　Not to a hero, statesman, chief alone,
But to a loving father, good and true,
　　To one in whom each kindly virtue shone?

How shall we mourn him? Bleeding hearts reply,
　　With all the silent eloquence of tears;

Feeling too deep for language, must deny
  The full expression of our griefs and fears.

How shall we mourn him? With a lofty trust;
  The Arm Omnipotent shall be our stay;
The cause in which he fell is good and just,
  And through the clouds, faith points to brighter day.

By REV. N. A. PRINCE.

WAIL not the dead, wail not the brave,
    Wail not the just, wail not the wise;
  Wail not the good, wail not the great!
The dead yet lives—heeds not the grave—
    Beyond the strife, beyond the skies,
    A martyr crowned in glorious state!
The chieftain sleeps, but millions wake;
    The night comes down, but hastes the morn,
    And drives his burning chariot far!
Th' oppressed rejoice, mad despots quake,
    Bright banners rise—the land adorn—
    And Freedom sings in every star.
Almighty God, eternal King,
    Whose wisdom guides, whose arm defends
    The nation in distress and fear,
Accept the love and praise we bring!
    On Thee alone our hope depends,
    Our Sun and Shield, forever near.

DE PROFUNDIS.

By JEANIE G———.

A SOUND of wailing fills the stricken land,
    O'er our bowed heads the waves of sorrow roll;
Justice and grief majestic, hand in hand,
    Intone a requiem for our martyr's soul.

A nation's heart bemoans the mighty dead,
    Reft in the hour of priceless victory won;
And Liberty, lamenting, droops her head
    Above the ashes of her noblest son.

The starry banner sadly floats above,
    The minute guns come booming on the ear;
Millions of hearts, o'er-charged with grief and love,
    Entreat to lay a flower upon his bier.

Behold the mournful pageant passing by!
    Our streaming eyes and quivering lips can tell
No purer soul have angels born on high
    Than his we loved so fervently and well.

Like incense wafted to the heavenly shore,
    Are loving prayers of those he died to save,
Whose clanking chains shall fetter them no more:—
    The ransomed freedmen bend o'er Lincoln's grave!

Weep, freedom! When in onward march of years,
    The pen of history tells the world his story;

Few, few can read the record but with tears,
  Though twined his name with an immortal glory!

Oh! tenderly we'll bear him to his rest,
  And plant rich seeds, with spring to rise in bloom;
They'll smile in dewy sweetness on his breast,
  Whispering, "RESURGAM" from the patriot's tomb!

By H. S. S———.

A NATION mourns to-day,
  Our hero-chief lies low;
Cursed be the hearts that planned the deed—
  The arm which dealt the blow.

We bow in reverent awe
  To God's supreme decree;
Unable now His ways to scan,
  His mighty plans to see!

Our grief no tongue can tell,
  Let traitors all beware;
The POISONED CHALICE that we drain
  May soon be THEIRS TO SHARE!

As one, each loyal heart
  Beats with fresh love to-day,
For him who through the storm and strife
  Has led us on our way.

Struck down by traitor hands,
    Thy spirit, kind and true,
Shalt hover o'er from shore to shore;
    Bid each his work to do.

Thine was a holy cause,
    And thine the heart to see;
While millions yet unborn shall bless
    The MARTYR FOR THE FREE!

Rest, weary pilgrim, rest!
    Thy "well done" work is o'er;
Amid the band, in angel land,
    Thou'lt REST FOREVERMORE!

ANONYMOUS.

MOURNFULLY, tenderly, bear on the dead;
    All his labors are ended, his spirit has sped,
Beyond the dark river, from confines of clay,
Upward to regions of unclouded day.

Mournfully, tenderly, solemn and slow,
Tears are bedewing the path as ye go;
Millions of freemen are mourners to-day,
Gently and gratefully, O bear him away.

Mournfully, tenderly, gaze on that brow,
Beautiful is it in quietude now;
One look, and then lay the revered to his rest,
A broad land of freedom begirding his breast.

Soon shall we bury him; up and depart
To life and duty with undismayed heart,
Fear not, for as sure as God dwells in the skies,
From the blood of our martyr fair harvests shall rise.

Peace, peace to thy spirit, thou servant of God,
The vale thou hast trodden, what numbers have trod,
Thou wilt greet them with joy in the kingdom above,
And thy crown will be fadeless through infinite love.

By C. D. G——

He wore nor crown nor purple; held no state
   Hedged by the spectre of the "Right Divine"
That haunts the visions of a kingly line:
He was his people's chieftain, and their mate;
Chosen from their midst as meet to bear the weight
Of office worthily; ay, more! approved
   By sorest trial steadfast to the trust
His worth had won! To save the land he loved,
   Amid the storm of strife, the heat of lust,
   And envy's gloom, and faction's blinding dust,
He kept the unflinching tenor of his path
   Towards its bright zenith—till the arch-fiend's spite
Belched, hot from hell, a minion of his wrath,
   With one fell blow to plunge a world in night!

By JOHN S. BENSON.

LIKE as th' fixed star shines constant in the skies,
    When night descending drives the sun to rest,
And beams benignly on uplifted eyes,
    As day, disrobed, lies slumbering in the west—
Like as th' fixed star unseated in the spheres
    And hurled to chaos, still leaves radiant trace
Of glory, lasting as the hoary years,
    Undimmed by ages, and unmissed in space;
So lived our President; as calmly great,
    A nation's sovereign orb, when robbed of day,
His lustrous soul the tranquil light of state,
    From veil of eve, till morn put on her ray.
So lived he—lives his fadeless reflex still,
    As centuries go round and cycles fill.

By A. McBOYLE.

DEAD! and a nation mourns to-day
    A great man slain by a traitor's hand;
Dead! oh our God! to Thee we pray:
    Thou hear'st the clang of tolling bell,
    The mournful cadence of its knell
    Speaks woe, but Thou do'st all things well.

Dead! in the zenith of his fame,
    When, under Thee, his patriot hand
Had well-nigh quenched rebellion's flame,
    That so hath scorched our bleeding land.

With heavy hearts and tearful eyes,
  To Thee a stricken people come;
Thou see'st their tears and hear'st their sighs;
    This woe that almost strikes us dumb
    Speaks in the hushed and silent hum
    Of minute gun and muffled drum.

Dead! warm-hearted, kind and true,
  Firm, faithful, honest, good and brave,
We little thought this April's dew
  Would damp our ruler's grave.

Dead! when the flag he loved so well
  In triumph waved; when coming peace
Seemed near to stay the troubled swell
    Whose waves have rolled from sea to sea;
    O God! whate'er Thy purpose be,
    Help us to be resigned to Thee.

San Francisco.

By S. G. W. BENJAMIN.

LET the nation weep,
  As they bear the martyr,
To his last, long sleep!

Ay, let the nation weep!
Another such as he
We nevermore shall see
This side eternity.

Ay, let the nation weep,
And let the slow bells toll
For the noblest soul
That ever dwelt in man,
Or ever led the van
Of Freedom's hosts to victory,
And rang the charge of Liberty.

Well may the nation weep
And shudder at the stroke
That all their slumbering wrath awoke.
What wretch so impious as to dare
To smite the leader of the people's choice,
Or seek to harm a single hair
Of him whose heart, whose hand, whose voice,
Were all employed to work the nation's good,
And stop the flow of fratricidal blood?
Perchance he did not seem
So great to those who deem
A traitor or a Nero
May still appear a hero,
If he but wear a classic face
Or ape the superficial grace
That marks the scion of a titled race;
Not such was he for whom we mourn;
From wealth or rank he was not born,
Nor heir to patrimonial lands
Tilled by the bondman's weary hands;
His was the celestial beauty
Of a soul that does its duty;

Noble patriot, husband, father,
He did not strive to gather
The laurels of a wild ambition,
That only yield a vain fruition.
To benefit mankind—this was his aim,
To labor and to live unstained with blame—
He died without a blot upon his name.
Let all the weary and oppressed,
From North and South and East and West,
For whom his great heart yearned,
For whom his spirit burned,
To give their sufferings rest,
Let all arise with lamentation,
And with his own beloved nation
Bequeath the fame
Of Lincoln's name—
A heritage for veneration—
To the remotest generation.

Ay, let the nation weep,
While the slow bells toll,
And the cannon roll
For the funeral knoll
Of his mighty soul!
Ye cannot break the slumber deep
That wraps his limbs in quiet sleep;
He cannot hear
The crowds that tread
Around his bier,
Nor see the tears they shed;

For he nevermore shall dwell
Among the people that he loved so well;
Let the nation's sorrow have its way
For him who was the nation's stay.

Our hearts are sad, our eyes are dim;
We hoped long years of rest for him,
To enjoy the peace for which he wrought,
The peace with his own life-blood bought.
But he has rest,
Among the blest,
And with the Christ he loved.
Enough—his work was done,
The victor's crown was won,
And God himself removed
The patriot-martyr to his home.
Enough—his task was done;
For us remains to guard his tomb;
To bid the willow wave
Around the sacred grave
Of him who loosed the slave,
And weave the fame
Of Lincoln's name
With that of Washington;
While kingdoms crumble, old and hoary,
In a world where all is transitory,
They shall ever shine, twin stars of glory,
With undimmed splendor, in our nation's story.

By MRS. GUSTAVUS REMAK.

WHAT mean these sad emblems of sorrow, so near.
    The deep wail of anguish—the eloquent tear?
The furling of flags by each patriot hand—
The echo of woe and dismay through the land?

Why falters our eagle, just soaring on high?
Why trembleth his bosom and dark grows his eye—
As though, while unfolding in gladness his wing,
He felt the sharp pang of a traitorous sting?

And why, where the altar of Liberty stands,
Is the goddess in tears?—why, with pale clasp'd hands
Is she kneeling imploringly, low at her shrine
Beseeching assistance and comfort divine?

Oh! woeful the tidings these symbols impart,
Oh, bitter the sorrow oppressing each heart!
The chief of our land has been cruelly slain,
And a nation of mourners is burdened with pain.

He is dead—who so earnestly strove for the right,
With conscience unsullied, and pure as the light
That glows from yon heaven!—or beamed from his eye
With the truth—he feared not for his country to die!

He is dead—a proud martyr for Liberty's cause,
The champion of freedom—unheeding applause:—

With his mantle of honor around him he stood,
His high, steady purpose—the country's best good.

He is dead—and for this we are mourning to-day,
For the friend of our country, so soon passed away;—
While—the olive branch clasped in his generous hand,
He was wooing the angel of peace to our land!

As the eagle, when seeking his eyrie on high,
Keeps his eye on the goal, as he soars through the sky;
So, on through the pathway to freedom he trod,
Just gained the bright haven, then passed on to God!

And now, though the stars on our banner grow pale,
And the music we hear is a funeral wail;
While millions are bending in tears o'er the sod—
Let us look from his grave to Omnipotent God!

God reigneth! Creator and Ruler of all,
Who permitteth "no sparrow unnoticed to fall:"
Whose love, from the clouds of the gloomiest night,
Unfoldeth the beams of His heavenly light!

The nation still lives! let this thought then inspire
A heartfelt devotion—a holy desire:
United in purpose and courage to be,
Till our land from the thraldom of treason is free!

Oh! then shall our banner unstained wave on high,
Our eagle exultingly soar through the sky;
Our land by the precepts of freedom refined
Be a beacon of light and of hope to mankind.

By REV. T. J. GREENWOOD.

TEARS! such as nations shed!
    Tears for our nation's head,
      In death laid low!
Bend 'neath our darkened skies;
Bend where our chieftain lies;—
Give forth your tears and sighs,
      In deepest woe!

Sudden the bolt that fell!—
Almost a nation's knell—
    From treason's hand!
Smiting our leader down,
When PEACE with olive crown,
Waited her sway to own,
    Over the land!

THOU, who in cloud and flame,
Writest Thy holy name,
    GOD OVER ALL!
Thou who in time of grief
Givest alone relief—
Let e'en our prayer be brief;
    On Thee we call!

Send Thou, O God, relief
To bosoms charged with grief,
    All they can bear!

Pity their keen distress—
The stricken widow bless,—
And the now fatherless,—
    Make them Thy care!

Quenched, though our nation's light,
Upward the spirit's flight,
    Trusting we bear!
Sod to its native sod,
Soul to its FATHER, GOD,
Home to its bright abode,
    On wings of prayer!

By Rev. SIDNEY DYER.

WEEP, oh land! 'tis manly weeping,—
    Every heart is bowed with grief;
Dead! oh dead! forever sleeping,—
    Noblest man, our martyred chief!
Earth ne'er heard such lamentation:
    Never man so vilely slain!
Wept by all, yea, every nation
    Thrills with one great throe of pain.

First of men, without ambition;
    Warring, yet revenge unsought;
Trusted, proved, in each condition,
    Noblest still in deed and thought,

Loving freedom,—millions freeing;
  For the truth he firmly stood;
Not a prophet, yet far-seeing,—
  Loving, honest, faithful, good.

Ruler, yet a loving brother,
  Winning with such guileless art,
That we loved him as another
  Washington, as great in heart.
Oh, what joy when re-confiding
  In that well-tried man, and true;
Well assured, his wisdom guiding,
  He would lead us safely through.

Soon the banner treason lowered,
  Proudly to the breeze unfurled,
Floats o'er Sumter's walls, restored,
  Stainless, to the wondering world.
Such his pledge when first invested
  With the sacred trust of power;
Four long years he never rested,
  Till we hailed the promised hour.

Oh, the rapturous, happy nation,
  He had guided through the fight;
Dreams of peace, a great ovation,
  Filled our souls through all the night.
What a fearful, bloody morning,
  Darker than night's shadows fled,
When the tolling bells at dawning,
  Woke the nation:—he was dead!

Still that great ovation keeping,
  Not with shouts, but tears of woe,
As, amidst a nation's weeping,
  Moves the funeral, sad and slow.
Bear him to his silent dwelling;
  Wreathe his fadeless diadem;
While our hearts, with sadness swelling,
  Chant his peaceful requiem.

Rest, thou mighty spirit, rest thee!
  All thy work on earth was done;
Soar where none will e'er molest thee;
  Wear the crown so nobly won.
Sacred amaranth entwining,
  Where thy cherished ashes lie;
In our hearts thy memory shining;—
  Freedom's martyr cannot die!

By Mrs. O. A. S. BEALE.

SILENT and mournfully,
  Lifting our eyes to Thee,
    Great God above!
Hear what our hearts would pray,
Touched by Thy hand to-day—
Fold this dark grief away,
    Under Thy love:

Slowly the midnight creeps!
Blindly the nation weeps
    Her idol slain!

Swifter than eagle's wing,
Light to our darkness bring!
Let freedom upward spring!
   Let justice reign!

Hushed our triumphant notes!
Shrouded, our banner floats
   Low o'er his tomb;
High as the angels tread,
God take our noble dead!
Crown his immortal head,
   Undying bloom!

Show us, O loving God!
Bending beneath Thy rod,
   All hearts as one—
Show us the light—the way!
Teach trusting lips to pray—
Our nation's heart to say—
   Thy will be done!

Thou art our country's hope!
Bear our proud banners up,
   With unseen hand!
Let every heart be strong!
Still shout the victor's song!
Each voice the strain prolong—
   "Our native land!"

By RUTH N. CROMWELL.

GIVE strength, O God! so many hearts
   Are prostrate in Thy sight,
Sustain with Thy o'erruling hand
   Thro' this our darkest night!

But yesterday our flags waved high,
   Their bannered stars unfurl'd,
Each cluster'd throng flashed forth the song—
   Glad tidings to the world!

But yesterday hope dwelt with us,
   Our solace and our shield;
And yesterday, she pitched her tent
   On every battle field!

She wrapped herself in starry robes,
   She bade our anguish cease,
While on her glowing brow she wore
   The olive branch of peace.

The gun lay muzzled at her feet,
   Sheathed was the flaming sword,
Our anthems reached Thy crystal gates—
   Hosanna to the Lord!

We laid our burden in the dust—
   We bade our wrath depart—
Our ships went freighted with the joy
   That thrill'd a nation's heart.

We worshipped Thee with feast and song,
  We said this dread shall pass;
The memory of this blood shall be
  Like dew upon the grass!

Oh! yesterday, so lifted up,
  So sacred in our might,
Give strength, O God! so many hearts
  Are prostrate in Thy sight!

Our flags are lowered on the earth,
  We stand abashed and still,
Our faded wreaths are thrust aside,
  O God! what is Thy will?

For Thou hast enter'd every door
  Within this stricken land;
Before their dead—confused, amazed
  The mighty millions stand!

We strive to utter forth our thought,
  Our words are weak and slow,
We strive to cover up our grief
  With the sumptuousness of woe.

Thanks to Thy grace, there needs no tongue
  The nation's heart to probe,
We need no Antony to show
  The dead man's gory robe!

High as the stars above our head,
  Broad as the land and sea,

Vast as the crime our souls deplore,
   So vast our grief shall be!

Oh, hapless land! how many years
   Of sorrow and of pain,
How much of life, and love, and joy,
   How much of waste and gain?

How much of sacrifice and tears,
   Of sun, and dew, and rain,
Ere time, God's comforter to man,
   Shall wash away thy stain?

By JABEZ M. FISHER.

AROUND Thy Throne, Almighty God,
   A weeping nation kneels this day;
Bending to kiss Thy chast'ning rod,
   Their heartfelt, sacred homage pay.

Grant comfort to the troubled heart,—
   Its lacerated feelings calm,—
Thy heavenly influence impart,
   Dispense Thy ever-healing balm.

Bright freedom's champion,—he who led
   The holy heaven-directed band
Of slavery's vanquishers, is dead,—
   Slain by a base assassin's hand.

Oh! reconcile us to the loss,
  Which we this day have met to mourn.
Teach us to bear the heavy cross,
  As by Thy blessed Son, 'twas borne.

Creator of the heavens above,
  We kneel before Thy awful throne,
To crave Thy holy care and love,
  And may Thy will O God, be done.

By GEORGE COOPER.

THE form that sped the Ship of State
  Mid storms which threatened to o'erwhelm,
Now stricken by the hand of hate,
  Lies dead beside the sacred helm!

Oh! lay him gently down to sleep,
  Beneath his hallowed western sod;
Toll, mournful bells! weep, nation weep!
  And leave the martyr to his God.

Now calmly moulder in the dust,
  The gentle heart, the kindly hand,
And purpose ever true and just,
  That freedom gave to all our land!

Our Father, hear a nation's prayer,
  And shield his loving ones who mourn!
Oh! heal the bruised hearts they bear,
  And from the darkness wake the dawn!

By Mrs. F. W. HALL.—Seventy Years of Age.

Yes! wreath the harp with summer flowers,
    Let music breathe her sweetest strain;
Let gladness wing the passing hours,
    For blessed peace returns again.

Long hath the war-cloud o'er us hung,
    And brothers met in murderous hate;
With anguish, countless hearts been wrung,
    'Til the whole land was desolate.

Our bright and starry banner flung
    Full to the breeze, floats broad and free;
And cannon's roar, and joy-bells rung,
    Proclaim a general jubilee.

    *   *   *   *   *

But hark! there falls upon the listening ear,
    A note of woe, a loud funereal wail!
Hushed are the sounds of mirth, the words of cheer,
    Brave hearts are bowed, and manly cheeks turn pale;
The very air seems heavy, and the gale
    Is burdened, with a rumor of such crime,
As well might seem incredible, in tale
    Of direst horror! all aghast we stand,
And feel that deeds most foul have stained our boasted
    land.

The nation's heart stands still! for he who stood,
    With strong right hand grasping the helm, but now

Guiding the Ship of State, amid the flood
  Of angry waters, falls beneath the blow
Of dark assassin; and our blessed bow
  Of promise fades,—a sombre dismal pall·
Envelopes all the land; and notes of woe,
  Rising and swelling where th' Atlantic roars,
  Blend sadly with the roar from broad Pacific's shores.

We mourn as for a father dead; nor we
  Alone; the wide, wide earth will feel the shock!
In his own hand he held the destiny
  Of millions; standing like a giant rock
Amid the breakers; though the foe might mock,
  False friends forsake, and many a hope deceive,
His heart was steadfast; nought his purpose shook;
  A fierce rebellion's mischief to retrieve,
  A country disenthralled and prosperous to leave.

Weep! ye oppressed of other lands, whose eyes
  Turn hopefully to this fair home of ours!
Seeming to your crushed hearts, a paradise,
  Where heaven its richest, choicest blessings showers;
Weep! as you see the cloud that darkly lowers
  On our horizon, late so heavenly bright!
He, who to freedom's cause, his noblest powers
  Untiring gave, hath fallen! in all time,
  There is no record of so damnable a crime.

In vain for us all nature smiles again,
  In vain the spring put on her brightest bloom;
A nation's tears are falling like the rain
  From summer clouds; we think but of the tomb

That soon will hold our mightiest. Is there room
    For aught but sorrow in our breaking hearts?
'Twere fit the landscape should be draped in gloom,
    When he, the loved and trusted one departs!
    So suddenly struck down, by death's unerring dart.

Now bear him to his rest, amid the tears
    And gratitude of millions; he hath gone,
While shouts of victory were in his ears;
    But green shall be his fame as years roll on;
Bright as the western sky at set of sun!
    His grave shall be an holy shrine, where we
May blend our sorrow-stricken hearts in one.
    O God of nations! in our agony,
    Help us to lift our smitten, fainting hearts to Thee.

By "MAY" OF SPARROWBUSH.—Thirteen Years of Age.

THERE are tears on all faces, in hearts there is mourning,
    And crape hangs in great sable folds at each door.
Weep, weep bereaved country! but though he has left us,
    We'll honor and reverence him evermore.

For coupled with God's it was his hand that led us,
    Safely and surely through war's troubled sea;
Seeing his way clear, while we were nigh fainting,
    He struck down the chains and the bondmen were free.

But now, when the war-clouds are constantly breaking,
   And the first joyous peace-beams are shedding their ray,
The assassin must come with the fatal-aimed bullet,
   And death, on his dark wings, bear Lincoln away.

If 'twere only our loss, then we might forgive him,
   But for every drop of the blood that he shed,
Our country's voice cries for ten times a full ransom,
   God's curse and a nation's rest on his base head.

Four long weary years did the trusted one labor,
   And never once during that time did he stray,
Unless it was when he would shield the wild traitor,
   From the vengeance of those, who their wrongs would repay.

Four years, and again he, the choice of the people,
   Was treading the path of his duty and care,
When suddenly torn from the head of the nation,
   But not from its heart, for he'll always live there.

Weep, Illinois, weep! for thy brave son has fallen,
   Bow thy sad head to the blow that has come;
But cherish the memory of thy departed,
   And joy, that thou ever couldst boast such a son.

And raising one hand to the heavens above thee,
   Vow that the death of the lost you'll avenge;
While from one end of the land to the other,
   Rises the wild shout, "Revenge! Revenge!"

COLUMBIA'S LAMENT.

By Miss EMMA H. BICKERSTAFF.

FAREWELL thou fond and true defender,
   Death has claimed thy precious form,
And this bleeding heart is riven,
   Bowed in grief before the storm;
Vain the cry that calls thee to me—
   Vain the pleading, yearning moan,
O, my Father! hast thou left me,
   Left thy child alone, alone?

When the fiends of dire rebellion
   Chained and bound me as their slave,
Crushed the Stars and Stripes of glory,
   Trailed in dust each silken wave—
When from lips of deadly hatred,
   Curses fell upon my brow,
Then you came to shield and guide me,
   Lead me safe—none knew nor how.

In my crown the stars are trembling,
   Somber light they shed for thee,
While the flag is mournfully floating
   Round my shoulders, sad and free.
Heavy is the pall that drapes it,
   Bringing anguish to the soul,
Blasting hope, and crushing gladness,
   Giving bells their solemn toll.

None will bless as thou hast blessed me,
  None so gently calm each fear,
None to lift the load, the burden,
  None to wipe the rising tear;
But upon thy grave I'll shed them,
  And bedew thy resting-place,
Bid farewell to love departed,
  Turn, and greet a stranger face.

In deep despair I linger near thee,
  Alas! those cruel words—good-bye—
'Tis Heaven's will—the cup so bitter,
  And thou didst for Columbia die.
Yes 'twas meet, our highest offering
  Was thy body, and it fell;
Sweet and peaceful be thy slumbers,
  Great and good, farewell, farewell.

ANONYMOUS.—English Paper.

"SIC SEMPER TYRANNIS!" the assassin cried,
  As Lincoln fell. O villain! who than he
More lived to set both slave and tyrant free?
Or, so enrapt with plans of freedom died
That even thy treacherous deed shall glance aside
  And do the dead man's will by land and sea;
  Win bloodless battles, and make that to be
Which to his living mandate was denied.
Peace to that gentle heart! the peace he sought
  For all mankind, nor for it dies in vain.

Rest to the uncrowned king, who, toiling, brought
  His bleeding country through that dreadful reign;
Who, living, earned a world's revering thought,
  And dying, leaves his name without a stain.

By P——, New Orleans.

TOLL bells! Your solemn funeral notes
  Keep proper music to our poor sad hearts.
Weep city! for the mighty hand that
Threw a shield around you,
Now lies stiffened; cold in death!
Hang out the sable drapery of woe,
And let the nation as a nation, weep
For one so mighty fallen.
O! choke not back the rising sob,
For none need be ashamed to-day
To let the waters of affection fall
Upon the new made grave
That covers all their hopes.
It is an honest grave—
An honest man who fills it.
O! bloody, bloody spectacle!
O! thrice accursed villain;
Our heads bow down in shame,
That one who claims a birth-right
With us all, could thus strike down
The nation's hope and trust.
    *   *   *   *   *   *

And this occurs, O, shame! beneath the arch
Of that proud Capitol they helped to rear,
And on whose dome the goddess of our nation
Stands to-day, pointing with her solemn finger
Upward to the spirits of the mighty dead,
Lost to us forever.
Men, patriots, brothers, rise!
Let not this damning deed go unavenged;
Let justice, hastened by the quickened pulses
Of our outraged hearts, seek out the guilty wretch,
And with a nation's awful rage,
Wreak vengeance on the parricide.
There's twenty million loyal hearts
Bound closely round with crape to-day.
They wait and watch, but mutter
Low and terribly, the word—*Revenge.*

ANONYMOUS.

TRUE patriot in the trial's heat,
   Where freedom's martyrs stood at bay;
Now proved commander gone to meet
   His "noble army" passed away.

But who shall bind the nation's wound?
   To whom again such love be given?
The voice that can with comfort sound
   Is only that of God in heaven.

By HARRY HAREWOOD LEECH.

OH bravest soul! oh wisest head!
    With gentle heart, and mercy's hand;
Why could ye not be spared to lead
    Thy people to "the promised land?"

We heard the music far away;
    We saw the flowers in their bloom;
The golden dawn of coming day
    Seemed not the night of coming doom.

But yesterday the bugles' blast
    Scarce drown'd the nation's joyous hum;
We knew the pangs, and deemed them past—
    We never heard the muffled drum.

We never saw the hidden hand,
    Nor heard the whispers in the wind;
"*Io Triomphe!*" through all the land,
    The laurel, olive, intertwined.

Our silken banners, wave on wave,
    Were floating in their native sky;
We did not heed the open grave,
    But pass'd the "dust and ashes" by.

We did not see the martyr-crown,
    The thorns were hidden near the rose;
And heads now bow most lowly down—
    Before the warning came the blows.

So near the people's heart, beloved!
　So simply grand, so nobly good;
To peaceful arts forever moved,
　Although the age was red with blood.

Thy memory will be the good
　That ever to a nation brings
God's purposes, so understood
　That men reach up to higher things.

And bondmen bless thee as they burn
　Rude altar fires by the way,
Embalming in a sacred urn
　The benediction of thy day.

By HENRY PYMN.

GOD bless Abraham Lincoln!
　A mourning people cry,
God bless Abraham Lincoln!
　The sighing winds reply.
God bless Abraham Lincoln!
　Is tolled from every spire,
God bless Abraham Lincoln!
　Trembles a nation's lyre.

At every fireside altar
　Is felt the stroke of death!
And God bless Abraham Lincoln
　Goes upon baby's breath!

For well he loved the people,
   And the people loved him well;
And every heart grows sick and faint
   As at a brother's knell!

A million knees are bended
   On southern plains to-day,
A million lips are quivering
   With words they cannot say:
A million broken voices
   Fill all the troubled air,
And God bless Abraham Lincoln!
   Is all their simple prayer.

My God, I humbly thank Thee
   Thou hast made this people one!
Henceforth we may not falter
   Till all Thy work be done!
For the haughty rebel spirit
   With lip that scorns and braves,
Still walks with proud defiance
   Above our soldier graves!

No more bludgeons in the senate,
   Nor whips for women's backs,
Nor daggers for the sick room,
   Nor hounds for human tracks.
No auction blocks for children,
   Of harem, or of home;
No murderers of Presidents
   In all the time to come!

No more of starving prisoners,
    Nor maiming of the dead,
But down, oh down forever,
    With slavery's hydra head;
For the people's voice is God's voice,
    And it thunders through the land:
"My mercy is my *justice*,
    And that alone shall stand!"

Oh pity for the wretched hand
    That laid the good man low,
But God forgive the guilty band
    That gave the work to do!
Perish! forever perish,
    The hand that stabs the state!
Nor think to turn God's lightnings
    By calling them man's hate!

Oh mourn him not, ye bondmen,
    Who died for you and me,
For our great liberator
    Is gone where all are free!
But bless the kind death-angel
    That gave his soul release,
And called the great peacemaker
    To go where all is peace!

Yes, bless the kind evangel
    That still would stay his wing,
Nor till the stars on Sumter rose,
    Would his great summons bring!

But when that rose-wreathed banner
  Proclaimed that all was won,
He called him quickly home to hear
  Servant of God, well done!

And now the hillsides burst with flowers,
  And birds in groves rejoice,
And God bless Abraham Lincoln!
  Ascends their mingled voice.
The rivers bear it to the sea,
  The sea to every clime,
Till God bless Abraham Lincoln,
  Is the universal chime!

A voice goes up to bless him
  From every soldier's grave,
While God bless Abraham Lincoln
  Cries the land he died to save!
And earth unites to bless him
  Through all her wide domains,
As up to God he humbly bears
  A million broken chains!

By Mrs. M. T. G. RICHARDSON.

HARK! a wail of lamentation
  O'er Columbia's land is borne,
Where the shout of exultation
Ran just now o'er victories won.
    All is sadness,
For the nation's friend is gone.

When disunion and secession
Glad would sever us in twain;
When the war-cloud brooded o'er us,—
Red and bleeding with the slain,
    All was darkness,
And a night of terror reigned.

Then a leader, kind and fearless,
Patriot, wise and true, God gave,—
Whose unfaltering, holy purpose,
Yet the nation's life may save.
    Freedom's champion,
Foremost 'mong the honored brave.

When our army all triumphant,
At the laurels victory won;
And thanksgiving, glad, exultant
Through each loyal heart had run,
    Traitors trembled,—
Then the assassin's work was done.

In the heart of this great people
Evermore shall be entwined
Memory of the martyred Lincoln,
Sacrificed at Freedom's shrine.
    Worthy offering,
Beacon light to all mankind.

By M. V. V——.

COME, citizens, around his bier,
   And look upon him where he lies!
Weep, freely, without shame or fear,
   These scalding tears which burn your eyes.
Weep, lest your hearts should rend asunder!
   Never, since the world began,
   Were such tears shed for any man
As these, which force themselves through rage and pain,
Like streams by earthquakes opened, or the rain
   That comes with peals of thunder.
Behold our murdered father, sent to sleep
   Before his night had come—behold, and weep!

Then, let your tears in wrath be dried;
   And here, beside his coffin swear
Fealty to that for which he died,
   And death to treason! Mutely swear
   An oath which naught can overbear:
By all the urgent past; by all
   The hurrying future, dare
To fix your will. Gaze on the pall
   Which covers him we love; behold, and swear!

By your deep pity for the woman,
   His widow, bringing home her dead;
And for his sons, too young for his inhuman
   Blow on their tender hearts; swear, by the red,

Deep stain of murder; more,
  By all our martyred dead!
Oh, swear by those whose nameless graves
  Cover our country o'er
With silent speech; and by the slaves,
  Whose eyes are turned on you in dread
    Of hope too great for gladness;
    By a world's sadness,
By the black folds through which our banner waves,
  By our past agonies of doubt and prayer,
By all our battle-fields, behold, and swear!

Oh, by those tortured heroes, changed,
  Through slow degrees to gibbering skeletons,
By hunger, frost, and mildew, unavenged
  Of us who heard, but heeded not, their groans;
    By earth's long dream of liberty,
    Which he was sounding to reality,
Who lies, the death-wound darkening there,
  Murdered—behold, and swear!

Swear by your own deep grief,
  Swear by your Christian's stern belief,
That he has perished, not in vain—
    That from his loss shall grow
  A great, immortal gain—
    That the base blow
Which leveled him shall set a people free—
  Shall loose the shackles on humanity—
    Shall open the blind eyes,
    And break the stubborn will

Of those who hinder, till the race shall rise
  Redeemed, and worthy of the sacrifice
Of him who lieth here, serene and still.

His work is ended. Ours is not yet done.
'Tis we must finish that so well begun.
He perished for the right: we dare
To live for it! behold, and swear!

By GEO. ALFRED TOWNSEND.

THE peaceful valleys reaching wide,
  The wild war stilled on every hand,
On Pisgah's top our prophet died,
  In sight of promised land.

Low knelt the foeman's serried fronts,
  His cannon closed their lips of brass,—
The din of arms hushed all at once
  To let this good man pass.

A cheerful heart he wore alway,
  Though tragic years clashed on the while—
Death set behind him at the play;
  His last look was a smile.

No battle-pike his march imbrued,
  Unarmed he went midst martial mails,
The footsore felt their hopes renewed
  To hear his homely tales.

His single arm crushed wrong and thrall,
   That grand good-will we only dreamed;
Two races weep around his pall,
   One saved, and one redeemed.

The trampled flag he raised again,
   And healed our eagle's broken wing;
The night that scattered armed men
   Saw scorpions rise to sting.

Down fell the brand in treason's hand,
   Its gashes as he strove to staunch,
And o'er the waste of ruined land
   To take the olive branch.

The holy crest by murder stained;
   Upon its shattered portal lie!
The test this bravo's lips profaned
   Be sanctified for aye!

In still green field or belfried kirk,
   Where'er high boughs his sleep may lull,
Here closed his life where closed his work—
   Beside the Capitol.

Be his tomb perturbed and pent,
   With no words, too weak for grief begilt;
Heap up his grander monument—
   The Union he rebuilt.

By H. WOODWORTH.

LINCOLN is dead! Oh, how those words of grief
    Proclaim a nation's loss, a nation's woe!
So deep an anguish as defies relief;—
    Lincoln is dead; and by the assassin's blow!

Weep, O, my country! it becomes thee now!
    Spare not thy tears,—in torrents let them flow;
Gird sack-cloth on, in dust and ashes bow!
    Lincoln is dead! and by the assassin's blow!

Thy noblest son is fallen;—thou should'st mourn
    As thou hast never mourned but once beside,
When he by whom thy infant flag was borne,
    Heard the dread summons, bowed his head and died.

Accursed treason! traitors most accursed!
    Ye have his death encompassed;—now prepare
To meet the storm that o'er your heads will burst;
    A storm of vengeful wrath, that will not spare!

'Twas reached, the limit of forbearance, when
    By the assassin's blow our Lincoln bled;—
Even the best, the most humane of men,
    By desperate wrongs to desperate deeds are led.

Henceforth no mercy for the traitors!—none!
    Deal them the death that they so madly deal!—
Sweep them from earth, till there remain, not one!
    Give them the halter, bullet, bombshell, steel!

There are some crimes that may not be forgiven,
  So damning in their guilt, so deep their stain!
They call for vengeance both from earth and heaven!
  Such is the deed by which was Lincoln slain!

Is there a man that breathes the Northern air,
  So vile, so fallen, lost to aught that's good,
As will with foul and traitorous lips declare,
  That he rejoices at that deed of blood?

Let him, too, suffer, for the day is past
  When northern treason can protection claim;
An outraged people will arise at last,
  And from our country wipe that brand of shame.

It was in Freedom's sacred cause he bled,—
  The noblest man of this, or any age,—
It will, the story of his death, be read
  In future days, on history's bloodiest page!

By Rev. THOMAS H. STOCKTON, D.D.

WITH humble heart and drooping brow,
  Before Thy throne, great God! we bow;
Earth's noblest state is naught but dust,
And Thou art all our souls can trust.

Not only fall the vile and vain,
Who seek no good, who soothe no pain;
But men whom angels must approve,
Whom nations bless, and Thou dost love.

For all he was of great and good,
We thank Thee in whose strength he stood;
For all he is we praise Thy name;
His rest is heaven, on earth his fame.

With him relieved, Thy work proceeds;
New hands shall emulate his deeds;
While still from heaven we hear his voice,
God reigns—let all the earth rejoice.

By C. C——.

OH, solemn march! on whose funereal state
  With mourning pageant, crowded cities wait;
Bear thou the mighty dead to honored rest
  Midst the fair meadows of those sunny plains,
    Where golden harvests shall around him wave;
  And glittering spires of peopled cities rise;
    Whose feet the many silvery rivers lave;
In that young empire of the fertile West
  That feels the pulses of her glad life chill
    With sudden grief, for him, her proudest son
Now to her arms returning, cold and still,
    From his high place of honor stricken down;
And hope and purpose, and life's generous glow
Quenched in an evil hour by one fell blow.

As falls the mountain pine, by lightning riven,
  As cleaves, from Alpine heights the ice-bound rocks;

As sinks the gallant ship, by tempests driven;
  Swift, as the ruin of the earthquake's shock,
Have, oft, the mighty fallen from height of power,
  Leveled to mortal dust by destiny,
  And earth beholds the pageant passing by,
The grief, the wonder of the fleeting hour.

Thus passed the pomp of Egypt's chivalry,
  Up from the red cliffs of the coral sea,
To Jacob's burial, midst those hills of bloom,
  That shed their crimson blossoms on the tomb
Where, laid in faith and hope, the patriarchs rest,
  While centuries their cycles long fulfill
In toil and bondage to their race oppressed;
  Till, led by Him who keepeth covenant still,
  Israel redeemed, his fatherland possessed.

So gazed the world when Asia's conqueror
  In triumph's joyous hour, by death o'ercome,
Passed from the splendor of the subject East
  To hold his little kingdom of a tomb,
In that memorial city by the Nile,
  A gold and purple show of royal state,
  Where Egypt's jealous care and worship wait,
And throngs the homage of each Grecian isle.

Heard ye the echo, borne across the wave,
  When France conveyed her cherished hero home!
From the lone exile of his island grave
  To rest in glory 'neath her proudest dome?

Along her vine-clad hills bright banners dance,
And rings the cry—Napoleon! *Vive la France!*
'Tis o'er, and Europe's conqueror, too, has won
His hour of triumph, and—an empty crown.

Build we memorial to our nobler dead?
   And shall th' eternal marble speak his fame?
Who lies entombed within the pyramid?
   Of all her ancient glory but the name
To Alexandria remaineth now;
   The rock wherein the patriarchs were laid,
Hath lost its sacred treasure long ago:
   We doubt the dim traditions of the place
So long by feet of desert wanderers trod.
   So perish monuments that man hath made,
But theirs is record, time cannot efface,
   Sealed with Jehovah's name, the friend of God.

Such record too is thine, oh noble life!
   On whose meridian darkens such eclipse
     As shrouds a nation in its sable pall!
   Thou, midst the discord, and the bitter strife,
    Hast looked in faith to Him who ruleth all.
Oh ruler, wise, magnanimous and good!
   We speak thy virtues now with quivering lips,
And learn the wisdom, then half understood,
   That, with unwavering purpose and strong hand,
   Has wiped the blot of slavery from the land;
   And built, in justice and in liberty,
   Enduring peace, and safe prosperity.

Soon fade the laurels conquerors have won,
  But thou, the' immortal amaranth shalt wear
  In courts of light, with nobler victors there,
Who cast their crowns before th' eternal throne.

Like him, who, from the height of Pisgah, saw
The land where Israel's wandering feet should rest;
And closed his eyes upon that vision blest :—
Buried by God upon that mountain lone,
A sepulchre no eye hath looked upon,
  Unvisited save by the winds of heaven ;—
  His time-enduring monument—the law,
  To him, amidst the clouds of Sinai given ;—
  His living record, through millenial years,
A people in its living memory bears.

By E. SHERMAN SMITH.

SLEEP ! martyred patriot, sleep !
  While mourning millions keep
Watch at the sacred portals of thy tomb ;
  Sleep on in peace profound,
  While, far and wide, resound
A nation's wild lamentings o'er thy doom.

  Sleep on ! and dream no more
  Of this most troublous shore ;
Let heaven's sweet rest for earth's sad wrongs atone :
  No foul assassin's hand,
  No traitor's murderous brand
Can reach thee in that realm to which thou'rt gone.

Rest! noble ruler, rest!
　　No care need vex thy breast
For the dear land which owned thy gentle sway;
　　Its night of woe is past,
　　Through clouds and tears, at last,
Dawns the soft promise of a happier day.

　　Sleep! for thy work is done,
　　And rest is fairly won—
Though all too soon thy noble heart was stilled;
　　Yet, may we joy to know,
　　Thou wert not stricken low
Till thy great mission here was well fulfilled.

　　Sleep! martyred patriot sleep!
　　The nation long shall keep
Most sweet remembrance of thy gentle worth.
　　Thy deeds, so wise and just,
　　Shall "bloom in the dust,"
And shed a living fragrance o'er the earth.

By CHRISTOPHER C. COX.

DEAD! Is he dead?
　　The nation's own President—he who to-day
Lived, breathed and acted—whose gracious sway
Won o'er the hearts of the loyal and true,
As he fought the great fight of his country all through,
　　Dead? Is he dead?

Startling the tale!
Not on his couch in the White House he lies,
Not of disease the great patriot dies,
Not by strange accident stopping his breath;—
Alas! none of these have consigned him to death.
Startling the tale?

Whence fell the stroke?
Stifling a life in its power and its pride—
A life for which thousands would freely have died—
A life the great nation so poorly could spare—
A life in whose deeds the whole world had a share—
Whence fell the stroke?

Tell the sad tale—
Waft it, ye swift winds, from city to plain,
Speed it, ye lightnings, from ocean to main.
Tell to the nation that he, their great head,
By the red hand of murder lies bleeding and dead!
Tell the sad tale.

Palsied the hand
That pointed the weapon—accursed be the heart
That prompted a crime at which devils may start—
And twice cursed the cause from which sprung the dark
    deed,
A natural shoot, as the fruit from the seed.
Palsied the hand.

Speak to all hearts:
Tell it in cottage, and tell it in hall,
The mighty hath fallen! The funeral pall

Lies draped o'er the form of the noblest and best—
A statesman, a hero, hath gone to his rest;
    Speak to all hearts.

    Hear—brave and true—
Curb the joy on your lips for the triumph ye've won,
Exult not awhile in the era begun;
Pause—weep bitter tears for the patriot gone,
Who led you through trial and victory on—
    Hear—brave and true.

    Listen, ye false;
Mantle your cheeks with hot blushes of shame,
Low bow your heads at the sound of his name;
Recall your dark treason and tremble to know
You nerved the foul murderer's arm for the blow!
    Listen, ye false.

    Toll the deep bell—
In symbols of grief throw the flag from its place,
Festoon cot and mansion from roof-top to base,
While thousands, with solemn, funereal tread,
'Mid silence and sorrow, bear slowly the dead—
    Toll the deep bell.

    He needs no tear.
Our banner droops low—our sky has grown dim—
We lament for ourselves, but, oh! friends, not for him.
Ripe with honors, his name by a million hearts blest,
The great work accomplished, he goes to his rest.
    He needs no tear.

There—let him sleep;
In his far distant home where a poor boy he came,
And won by his worth the proud title to fame;
Another Mount Vernon, his grave in all time,
The Mecca for pilgrims of every clime.
There—let him sleep.

The seal has been set—
Go, bend o'er the turf where he slumbers alone,
And "Abraham Lincoln" carve deep in the stone,
The mortal remains turn to dust where they lie,
But the noble old President never can die!
The seal has been set.

By PEREGRINATOR.

AJAR thy gate, celestial dome;
Behold! angels and archangels guide
Reviver of a nation home!
Among the just, on time's continual change,
His name shall proudly move,
As pole-star of Republic's range,
Mighty champion, freedom's son.

Longevity denied by traitors' wild, malignant rage,
In midst of high, most noble deeds,
None have surpassed on history's page:
Calm, comprehensive soul, whose kindness swayed
O'er tribes, e'en nations at their birth,
Love, charity and truth its fountain made,
Nations shall mourn his sad, untimely flight from earth.

Although now dead—shot down at night,
He left behind the ruling chart
To guide the world to right;
And from his dust there shall arise
Some valiant sons to grasp his creed with might,
And gain triumphantly the prize.

But hark! methink the nation's voices ring
With anger, mingled with contempt—
For retributive justice bring,
To crush the dire infatuated fiends.
Now tremble, leaders of rebellion's host,
And view the yawning woe Pandora planned,
To ingulf you and your vaunted boast.

And now, O, ye sons of darker hue—most loyal hearts—
Droop ye, alarmed, for fear
His loss has spent your legal part?
No, no; look up to Him whose spangled lights adorn
Yon vaulted heavens above:
He will surely break a brighter morn,
To crown the triumph of His love.

California.

By G. MARTIN.

TO-DAY the dumb and dismal tomb
Conceals him in his depth of gloom,
And while its shadows round him close,
His myriad friends, and sullen foes,
Stand darkened in the dread eclipse;
And breaking hearts, through ashen lips,

Murmur in sobs—'tis all they can—
The world has lost an honest man.

Pure patriot! uncomputed, rare,
The world could ill afford to spare
The sum of goodness lost in thee,
And hence our great calamity.

Throughout all nations—everywhere,
But most where freedom's blessed air
Expands the honest Briton's soul,
Swift as the mournful tidings roll,
At sumptuous board and humble hearth
Will cease the wonted sound of mirth,
And indignation, grief, and tears
Will shake the fathers white with years,
And wring the matrons' hearts, and pain
The instincts of the youthful train;
And all the toiling, trusting host,
Who had most cause to love him most,
Will think, as from a blow they bend,
We've lost a father, brother, friend.

This scanty verse I fain would lay
Upon thy bier, my friend, to-day;—
My friend, because my early years,
Through poverty, and toil, and tears,
Glimmered upon the world, and wrought
Within my boyish brain the thought,
That, somehow, there was something wrong,
The people weak, and yet so strong;

And, groping in that early dream,
I saw the truth at distance gleam.
If all who work would but unite
To set some monstrous ills to right,
The gifts that now exalt the few
Would raise the squalid millions too.
And this fresh hope, my young ideal,
Is in our western world made real.
Here liberty at length released
From persecuting king and priest,
From slavery's thrall, and treason's power,
Lifts, in this sacrificial hour,
Her snowy hands to heaven, and cries,
" Rise up, my mourning children, rise!
His task was done, his battle won,
And I can spare my youngest son."

Montreal.

By L. J. CIST.

"This Duncan
Hath borne his faculties so meek—has been
So clear in his great office, that his virtues
Will plead like angels, trumpet-tongued, against
The deep damnation of his taking off."

OH mournful night! of all beside,
   The dismalest and saddest!
Since erst to Him, the crucified,
   A dark farewell thou badest!
Oh, fitting day for such a deed,
   The christian world appalling—

The martyr's crown upon his head
   So unexpected, falling!

The kindest heart in all the land!
   The bravest and the truest!
The only one, perhaps, to stand
   Against our danger newest—
That hatred and revenge shall be
   Henceforth, our rule of action;
Who will so wisely steer, as he,
   From all th' extremes of faction?

Oh, woe the day! Oh, woe the hour!
   Accurst the bloody traitor!
Whose desperate deed of deadly power
   Has op'd the burning crater
Of passions fierce—subdued of late—
   The surface underlying,
To spread—*a lava flood of hate*
   And bitterness undying!

Was there *not one* in all the land,
   (If victim we must offer,)
Of those who stand a patriot band,
   Ready their lives to proffer—
Would *no one else* suffice?—no blood
   Save *his* appease his haters?—
So kindly good, that still he stood
   Best friend to foes and traitors?

Honest and true!—His self-distrust,
   His kindness and meekness—

His *very virtues* verged almost
  Upon the edge of weakness!
No bitterness upon his lip,
  And in his heart no malice,
For that hate's draught he might not sip.
  He thrust aside the chalice!

'Tis hard that he, who four long years
  Had borne the toil and burden,
Should die, just as in sight appears
  The end—his sole-sought guerdon;
Rebellion crushed, with peace sincere—
  Our Union's restoration,
And, entering on its new career,
  A great, united Nation.

But ours the loss, and his the gain!
  His record's now immortal!
Nor would we call him back again
  On this side death's dark portal.
His work is done! His fame is won!—
  In proud Columbia's story,
Her *first* and *second* Washington
  Together linked in glory!

St. Louis, Mo.

TREASON'S MASTERPIECE.

By GEO. VANDENHOFF.

TREASON has done his worst!
    A hand accurst
Has made the nation orphan by a blow;
Has turned its hymns of joy to wail and woe
As for a father lost, a saviour slain,—
And blood, and toil and anguish spent in vain!

    Half his great work was done,
      By victory won
O'er recreant chiefs, and rebels in the field,
Compelled to bow the knee and homage yield;
And his calm breast, from war and vengeance turned,
With generous pity towards the vanquished yearned.

    Deep joy was in his soul
      As o'er it roll
Sweet thoughts of peace and magnanimity,
Wounds healed, wrath quelled, his country free,
Foes turned to friends, the bitter past forgiven;—
Such thoughts as earthly power make like to heaven.

    While all suspicion slept,
      The assassin crept
Into the circle where, in guardless state,
The simple chief in friendly converse sate,
And, in an instant, ere a hand could rise,
The nation's hope a slaughtered martyr lies!

In peace, great martyr, sleep!
    Thy people weep,
But stop their tears to swear upon thy grave,
The cause thou died'st for, they but live to save;
And the great bond, cemented by thy blood,
Shall stand unbroken, as it still hath stood.

    The traitor's fiendlike act,
    By stern compact,
Binds us still closer 'gainst the murderous band
That fain with blood would deluge all the land;
But vanquished by the sword, for mercy kneel,
And pay it, granted, with the assassin's steel.

    Oh, for this hellish deed,
    Thousands shall bleed,
That else had lived to bless thy gentle name
By mercy wreathed with an immortal fame;
And traitors, from a nation's wrath, shall learn
That outraged pity's tears to sternest justice turn!

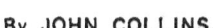

By JOHN COLLINS.

THE nation mourns—ay, bleeds with sorest grief,
    No tongue may now our bitter sorrow tell;
The breaking heart can only find relief,
    In those few words, "He doeth all things well."

Weep that a prince in Israel is gone;
    Faithful, like him, the Hebrew sire of old,

Weep, for the immortal dead who stood alone,
   Endowed with virtues of no common mould.

As some tall cliff upon the sea-beat shore,
   Unmoved, resists the wave and howling gale,
Nor strife of tongues nor din of murderous war,
   To foil his noble mission, could avail.

Weep for the kindest heart! now stilled in death;
   Lenient to crime—to misery, ever dear;
A wail of anguish comes from earth beneath,
   And heaven drops down a sympathetic tear.

Mourn for a statesman, lost to all mankind—
   A patriot pure, by love of justice led;
Genius, and worth, and intellect combined—
   Weep for our truly loved and honored dead.

Let every bell toll mournfully the knell
   When thousands stand around his open tomb,
Till eyes with tears and hearts with sobbing swell,
   And heads are bowed in universal gloom.

Let muffled drums the solemn tones repeat,
   In rolling thunder, heard from sea to sea,
And flags be draped when sorrowing millions meet,
   While the world stands in silent sympathy.

Weep for the good, struck down in manhood's prime,
   Dying, all senseless, by the murderer's hand,
A glorious martyr for his faith sublime,
   Time-worn and travelling to a better land.

That noblest blood has not been shed in vain!
  For every drop a million tears shall flow;
A million hearts be leagued to strike again
  The secret traitor or the open foe.

Who shall not love and venerate thy name?
  Hope of the nation in her darkest hour,
Inscribed forever on the roll of fame,
  "The guardian of her glory and her power!"

Praise to thy memory be in coming years
  That thou hast dared the bondmen to defend,
When every dusky brow shall bless with tears,
  And, kneeling, thank God for the "Freedman's Friend."

Blest shade of Lincoln! thou hast fought the fight,
  Maintained the faith and now the crown hast won;
Rest thee in heaven! on earth, with proud delight,
  Men shall revere our "second Washington."

The Father of his Country, lived and died,
  From foreign foes the commonwealth to save,
Thine was the glorious task, to his allied,
  By freedom's hands to dig rebellion's grave.

While history smiling bids the western world
  With glowing pride its "PATRIÆ PATER" see,
She bends to meet thee, with our flag half furled,
  And sighs, thine, PATRIÆ SALVATOR, be."

Departed spirits of our fatherland,
  Ye who have toiled, and watched, and wept, and prayed,
Firm as a storm-defying rock, shall stand
  The blood-sealed Union that your hands have made.

If to the souls in bliss 'tis ever given
  The dark eventful scenes of earth to know,
Look down, immortal patriots, from heaven,
  As guardian angels of your land below.

By FLORY FAVORITE.

IN this dark hour, O God,
  We need such help as Thine;
Our mourning spirit fain would ask
  Encouragement Divine.

A nation bathed in tears,
  A people sore distressed,
Look through the grim and crowding fears,
  To Thee, O God, for trust.

Around the tear-stained bier
  Of him, our nation's pride,
We kneel in deep humility,
  Nor seek our grief to hide.

No more a million tongues
  Give praise for victories won;
Trophies of war unheeded go,
  And at our feet are strewn.

All, all is dim and drear,
    And o'er our nation's path,
We nothing see but threatening clouds
    Of war's unchristian wrath.

We need Thy heavenly aid
    To help our trust secure—
We need the power of Thy will
    That we may yet endure.

Oh, teach our hearts to wear
    The shield of fortitude—
Teach us to feel that trouble comes
    Laden with lessons good.

And, leaning on Thy arm,
    In Thee we will confide;
For even midst afflictions dread,
    We feel Thou'rt on our side.

By DENNIS B. DORSEY.

SLOWLY we come to learn thy worth,
    Oh, genial man! oh, modest sage!
Slowly we come to see we've lost
    The grandest spirit of the age.

So near we felt the loving heart,
    Gentle and warm tow'rd all mankind,
We ne'er looked up to see ourselves
    O'ershadowed by the mighty mind.

Now scarce we know which we most miss,
  The leader's mind or brother's heart;
And scarce we know which most we prize,
  The brother's love or leader's art.

The world with us will prize them both;
  To us alone they were not given;
Like light and air, to all mankind,
  They were a common gift of Heaven.

Not we alone thy death deplored,
  Not we alone thy absence weep;
The world through all the ages hence
  Thy name shall love, thy fame shall keep.

ANONYMOUS.

AMERICA, mourn!
  Thy grief, thy tears, are well,
    So toll the passing bell:—
  Thy beautiful locks are shorn;
Locks of thy strength and crown of thy deep night—
    Oh beautiful and bright!
Shorn as the morn was breaking, and the star
Of peace was rising o'er the front of war;
And for the moment, like a giant slain,
Thy stout young limbs lie paralyzed with pain
And a great cloud of woe on all things falls,
Clothing a continent in funeral palls.
    Toll, toll the passing bell!

Man of the people, father of the state!
   Shall we not weep for thee?
   Woe is me! woe is me!
Our hearts are burdened with a very great
   Sadness we cannot cast away;
   For, in the very zenith of our day
Of joy triumphant, such as nation never
   Had cause to know before,
The rage of hell thy royal life did sever,
And stole thee from us to another shore.

   Would God had passed the cup!
   But let His will be done,
   Still must our tears well up,
   Great heart, for like the sun,
Thy gentle face did melt us, and just things,
More kindly thoughts, and mercy all divine,
Were working in us like a holy wine,
   Soothing the many stings—
Withdrawing one by one the cruel darts
War had left quivering in our bleeding hearts.

   Wail, children of the dark!
Your more than father has forsaken you.
   Wail, rebel men and states!
   Your shipwrecked bark,
Spotted with untold murder, he'd have saved.
Him ye have slain who would have changed your fates.
   Laws and evangels new,
   Ye have called down and braved;

Woe! woe! hath God but mercy for his shroud,
Or justice, also, hidden in the cloud?

   Wail, people of the main—
All ye oppressed, for him your captain slain!
   For him who, with strong hands,
Broke from four million slaves their cruel bands;
   Who, with unselfish aim,
Simple and honest as a little child,
  But with a godlike trust and flame,
Breasted the fury of rebellion wild,
  Withstood the wiles of tyranny and wrong,
Upheld the flag of liberty and right,
   Through unexampled night;
And died so sadly, just as the glad song
   Of triumph in our wars,
From twice ten million throats, was ringing to the stars.

   Sire, shall we call thee great?
It suits thee best to call thee wise and good,
The Moses who did lead us through the flood,
  Redeemer of our statesmanship and state.
Thou didst make office honorable. With thee
  The king was swallowed in the man. Thy great
Soft eye was full of human sympathy
  Thy acts made good. Thou hadst no room for hate;
And, like the Christ, thy orb in ocean dips,
Forgiveness dropping from thy loving lips.

   Still we must needs
Mourn, for the heart of hearts within us bleeds,

But not so much for thee;
Thy martyrdom for liberty
Has sealed thy glory, made thy name and fame
A beacon light,
An ever burning flame,
Nor tyranny, nor time can pale.
Thy star of splendor rises o'er the night
Of centuries past, and centuries to be,
With a broad blaze which all the world shall see;
And seeing, worship next to Deity,
Lincoln, the just, all hail!

By JAMES M. STEWART.

LET the President sleep!—all his duty is done,
He has lived for our glory, the triumph is won;
At the close of the fight, like a warrior brave,
He retires from the field to the rest of the grave.
Hush the roll of the drum, hush the cannon's loud roar,
He will guide us to peace through the battle no more;
But new freedom shall dawn from the place of his rest,
Where the star has gone down in the beautiful West.
Tread lightly, breathe softly, and gratefully bring
To the sod that enfolds him the first flowers of spring;
They will tenderly treasure the tears that we weep
O'er the grave of our chief—let the President sleep.

Let the President sleep—tears will hallow the ground,
Where we raise o'er his ashes the sheltering mound,
And his spirit will sometimes return from above,
There to mingle with ours in ineffable love.

Peace to thee, noble dead, thou hast battled for right,
And hast won high reward from the Father of Light;
Peace to thee, martyr-hero, and sweet be thy rest,
Where the sunlight fades out in the beautiful West.
  Tread lightly, breathe softly, and gratefully bring
To the sod that enfolds him the first flowers of spring;
They will tenderly treasure the tears that we weep
O'er the grave of our chief—let the President sleep!

By JAMES RISTINE.

TREAD slowly, reverently, ye
    Who bear the great man to his grave,
For the world and coming centuries see
    These plumes and funeral garlands wave.

In veneration bow the head,
    For 'twas a patriot and sage,
And the lustre of his life will shed
    Fresh glory on his land and age.

Large in the love of all mankind,
    And of reform intelligent,
Through storied past ye may not find
    Such virtue on high purpose bent.

To break the fetters from the slave,
    And brush away the captive's tear,
A broad soul's energy he gave,
    And gave the corpse on yonder bier.

'Twas his to spurn aspiring guile,
  And cherish to his heart alone,
The exalted duty that may smile
  Unmingled with a patriot's moan.

'Twas his to spurn the partisan aims
  That thirty perilous years had reared,
And turn to the majestic names
  The world has honored and revered.

He, threw his full heart's sympathies
  Around a nation whelmed in grief,
And helmsman on the tossing seas,
  He freed the ship from shoal and reef.

And when uprisen justice sought
  To tread the mutinous hearts to earth,
And reassert the truth it taught,
  When the old victorious flag came forth,

He stood before the eager sword,
  And checked the cannon's mouthing hate,
That harmony might be restored
  With blessings to each bleeding state.

And yet the traitor's dripping hand,
  Red with the stain of brother's blood,
Brought deeper sorrow to the land.
  The kind, the gentle, and the good,

The warm, forgiving heart was stilled
  By the assassin's coward stroke.

But though with mourning it has filled
　　The nation's breast, it has awoke

The vengeance of a noble race,
　　And thousands yet to earth shall reel,
Ere truth the double crime efface,
　　With fearless musketry and steel.

On tablets of the people's heart
　　The records of his deeds will rest,
And when they muse of him, will start
　　Afresh, the tears that bathe his breast.

With Washington his name shall stand,
　　As, LINCOLN, THE GOOD PRESIDENT,
Who hurled rebellion from the land,
　　And healed the wounds that strife had rent.

And springs shall come and go, with flowers
　　And blossoms in the lucent air,
To deck the shrine of wintry showers,
　　And forests moaning like despair;

And the dread gloom of conflict part,
　　And come the happy smile of peace;
And discord leave the rankling heart,
　　And reason the shut mind release;

And then shall they who hail his doom
　　With gladness, bless the honored name,
And drop, repentant, at his tomb,
　　The tears that seal his patriot fame.

OURS THE CROSS; THINE THE CROWN.

By Mrs. R. A. CAMERON.

YES, "ours the cross," lamented dead,
    And thine the starry crown;
For thou hast ceased the weary fight,
    Thou'st laid thine armor down.
A diadem of light now rests
    Upon thy regal brow;
The struggle o'er for thee at last,
    A victor crowned art thou.

Yes, "ours the cross"—not flower-crowned—
    We still must journey on,
We still must wage the fearful fight
    Till victory is won.
But thou hast passed earth's cloudy vale,
    And peace and joy are thine—
Thou'rt resting, all thy labors o'er,
    In the arms of Love Divine.

Thine was a brave, heroic soul,
    Of more than mortal mould;
Within it dwelt all pure designs
    And mercies thousand-fold.
The angels' song, "Peace and good-will,"
    Fell on thy listening ear,
And in thy heart its melody
    Waked echoes sweet and clear.

That rarest trait, forgiveness, shone
   Through all thy noble life,
And breathed its holy influence o'er
   The last of earth's sad strife.
With blessings for thy fallen foes
   Thou laidst thy great life down—
Yes, "ours the cross," brave, noble soul,
   And thine, the starry crown.

A glorious crown to thee is given,
   Our nation's hope and pride—
For freedom's holy cause alone
   A martyr thou hast died!
In thy rich manhood's prime, thy soul,
   That well earth's ways had trod,
Loosing its drapery of flesh,
   Went peacefully to God.

Thy name enshrined shall ever be
   In every patriot heart—
Heavy the task 'twas thine to share,
   And nobly borne thy part.
A nation free shall send thy name
   Through coming ages down—
Thank God, though ours may be the cross,
   Thine is the victor's crown!

Yes, "ours the cross, and thine the crown,"
   Brave, noble, patriot soul!
Why do we mourn? The battle's past,
   And thou hast reached the goal!

No more the anxious load for thee,
   No more the weary strife,
Thou'rt passed from sin and suffering here
   Into the perfect life.

Thank God that peaceful rest is thine,
   Now earth's last work is o'er,
The blissful rest of heaven and home
   Upon the shining shore.
And when our life-work, too, is done,
   We lay our armor down,
May we, our crosses left behind,
   Like thee, receive our crown.

Brashear City, Texas.

By J. G. FIELD.

FIVE years ago you laughed with us,
   Were glad when we were gay;
But times have changed, and we are sad—
   So sad with you to-day.
And men are pale at news so dread—
Lincoln and Seward wounded—dead!

Four days ago the cannon's roar,
   Of peace the welcome sign,
With sound so grand and joyous came
   Booming across the line.
To-day bells toll in many towers;
Tolling on your side, tolling on ours.

Tolling for the noble dead—
   Lincoln, loved so well.
Oh! we grieve with you to-day;
   Words can hardly tell
How our thoughts with horror creep,
And men are not ashamed to weep!

Canada.

By EMILIE LAWSON.

TOLL for the dead!—dead ere the work was ended!
   For a mighty man laid low,
   And a nation full of woe!
But chime! chime for a king Godward ascended!

Chime for the king whose name no shadow staineth!
   Who bore the people's cross,
   Counting their loss his loss;
But toll! toll that this cold clay is what remaineth!

Toll for the warm heart stilled; the kind lips breathless;
   For the father and the friend,
   Toll till all time shall end!
But chime for the great soul, unfettered—deathless!

Nature's beloved guest! born in a forest,
   Where whispers of the wood
   Taught him love's brotherhood;
And dead!—dead when his wise hand is needed sorest!

Toll! for the nation's heart of hearts is shaken;
    While vengeful voices cry
    In fury to the sky,
Justice is man's! and earth is God-forsaken!

Have we forgotten the Lord in our poor blindness?
    Over the infinite dark,
    Can He not guide our ark,
Who calls His faithful pilot in His kindness?
<small>San Francisco.</small>

By CHARLES W. REED.

THE church-bells swing above our heads, the heroes'
    cause is won;
We'll praise our God with joyful shouts for what His
    hand hath done;
He built us walls on either side: the dark Red Sea
    of blood
Daunts us no more, for treason lies engulfed within
    its flood.

What though the night was long and dark, though
    war-clouds brooded high?
What though we shrank from widow's tear and orphan's
    stricken cry?
The cloud of fire moved at our front, his hand had
    placed it there;
We trod behind with steady steps, faith hand in hand
    with prayer.

A light was spreading in the east, it broke along the
    sky;
As vampyres flee at morn's approach, we saw the
    traitors fly;
And as they fled like morning mists before the rising
    sun,
We lost our noble cloud of fire; its destined work was
    done.

Weep not, O nation, for thy loss; God doeth all things
    right;
We do not need the cloud of fire when He has banished
    night;
But praise Him as we hail the glow of victory's gor-
    geous sun,
That He took the workman not away until his work
    was done.

Give praise to God, His chosen saints, the land is pure
    and free!
O may His grace now stir the earth as tempest shakes
    the sea!
His hand hath held our banner up, hath saved each
    stripe and star;
Oh let us cluster round His cross, His watchmen call to
    war!

With hands outstretched, on Zion's hill we marshal
    for the fray;
Give now, O God, the strength of steel to feeble tools
    of clay!

Let Satan's walls fall in the dust, as in Thy name we
    come,
And when our toil is finished here, take all Thy work-
    men home.

ANONYMOUS.

WHEN raging earthquakes bury towns,
    Or fierce volcanoes lash their manes
Of boundless, fiery ruin round
    The groaning hills and shrieking plains,
The world may fitting emblems find
    To speak the horror of its heart,
In cities craped, in banners furled,
    And all the solemn show of art.

But when a human hand is turned
    Into a ruthless demon-power,
And smites a nation in its chief,
    Even at his triumph's crowning hour,
What emblems shall man fitting find,
    What types sad, grand enough to show
The horror shaking continents,
    And their infinity of woe?

Alas! alas! we wildly feel
    There should be still some outward sign,
And so we furl the shining flag
    And darkly cloud the glowing shrine.

How vain! At last the nation lifts
   Its naked hands to heaven, and owns
The impotence of every type
   Before the awful throne of thrones:

Then silent stands and thinks of him
   The swerveless good, the calmly great:
In wonder would the treason pierce
   Of their beloved's mystic fate.
Was he too dear an idol here?
   Too merciful for this dread time?
Did Heaven now will a sterner hand,
   With justice mailed, to guard the clime?

O God of nations, if we sin
   In questioning, forgive, for we
Are by our woe driven to seek
   The meaning of eternity!
Forgive, and bless, and make us feel
   That Thou wilt still love, watch, save all,
Though even the best of rulers die,
   Though earth should sink and planets fall!

By UNA.

THE shouts of triumph, loud and long,
   Ring forth throughout the land;
The Union's sons so brave and firm,
   In hosts exulting stand.

War's dense, black clouds are cleft in twain,
   The clear, blue sky's between,
Enamelled in the azure heaven,
   Our dear "old flag" is seen!

All nature smiles—the earth is glad—
   The song of freedom sounds!
Her sons appear in laurel decked,
   With joy the air resounds.

But hush! amid triumphant notes
   There comes a mournful wail;
Smiles change to tears, and brave hearts break,
   A nation's brow is pale.

Lo! as the lovely bird of peace
   Soars high, with wings outspread,
Her pinions fall, she fainting droops—
   The President is dead!

He who hath steered our Ship of State
   Through fierce ungrateful wrath,
Safely o'er treason's boiling waves,
   To truth's smooth, tranquil path,

Is stricken down by murderous hands—
   Oh! parricidal crime!
Earth stands aghast at such a deed,
   Unparalleled in time.

In sable hues we shroud our flag,
   In sackcloth veil its stars,

He loved it so; if it could weep
  'Twould mingle with our tears.

The nation's father—ever true
  Was the illustrious chief—
We mourn our loss in deep distress,
  With stern indignant grief.

Thou martyred one, Columbia weeps
  In anguish o'er thy tomb;
But shining angels welcome thee
  To a celestial home!

God of our Fathers! Thou who gav'st
  This second Washington
Oh! guide us in this mighty work
  Which he had well-nigh done.

Gird up the nation's fainting strength,
  Solace her bleeding heart,
And wisdom to her noble sons
  Do Thou by grace impart.

New Orleans.

By G. MARTIN.

WHILE swells the unusual wail,
  In heart-gusts, o'er the murdered man,
His life, my wounded soul, unveil,
  His entrance and his exit scan;
For as in Timnath Samson drew
  Sweets from the noble lion dead,

So may a living soul renew
    Its vigor from the martyr's bed.

Dimly within the western woods,
    Where Indiana smiles, we see
A peasant boy, whose thoughtful moods
    Still bear him onward hopefully.
With heart benevolent and blythe,
    Which aches but at another's pain,
He wields the axe, the hoe, the scythe,
    Singing the glad songs of freedom's reign.

And when to manhood grown, full taught,
    By rushing flood and winged wind,
What freedom meant, one holy thought
    Ruled paramount within his mind.
That thought was—justice to the slave,
    Leading to words and acts sublime,
And musings how he yet might save
    His country from her shameful crime.

At length a statesman, rough, but true,
    Anon Columbia's chosen chief,
He stands, and in the world's broad view
    Declares his purpose, firm and brief.
The hour of trial hastens fast—
    Rebellion's roar, and battle's shock;
He meets the suffocating blast,
    And stands unmoved, a granite rock.

Seven crimson seasons o'er him roll,
    And treason, rampant, stands at bay;

But with a calm, unshrinking soul,
   In heaven he trusts, and leads the way.
In patriarchal tones he speaks,
   And from a million swarthy limbs
The chains fall off—oppression shrieks—
   And liberty sings glorious hymns.

And as the bellowing strife prevails,
   The star-led world looks on amazed;
But right, oft baffled, never quails,
   The rebel crew reel backward, crazed.
And in the dust their banner lies,
   Trampled and torn—no more to shame
The light of the eternal skies
   With slavery's accursed name.

His country's saved, his work achieved,
   He boasted not of what he'd done,
But rather, in his goodness grieved
   For all sad hearts beneath the sun.
For even his most malignant foes,
   Blind perverts! whom he sought to save
From ruin's toppling crash; their woes
   He pitied, and their faults forgave.

And now his genial spirits seek
   Their wonted channel—war's fierce rage
Had surged against his pallid cheek,
   And multiplied the signs of age.
A moment's respite from the storm,
   A little rest from goading care,

His people fain to see his form
    Where mirth and music thrill the air.

Beside him smiles his loving wife,
    Leaning upon the honored man
Whose life to her is more than life,
    Who feels as only woman can.
Guileless himself, he could not think
    That treason's foulest whelp had power
To push him off from earth's dim brink
    In such a place, at such an hour.

Behind him glares the demon eye,
    Behind him moves the demon hand,
A quick, sharp sound—a start, a cry!
    Then gleams aloft the hellish brand.
'Tis done! his venerable head
    Sinks peacefully—his soul departs;
The honest President is dead,
    And with him die all human hearts.

Go, student of the vanished years,
    Compare the democratic sage,
Whose exit leaves the world in tears,
    With the crowned sons of every age.
His humble birth with theirs compare,
    His labor 'gainst their leisure weigh;
Mark well how, shunning every snare,
    He kept the straight and narrow way.

Draw thence this lesson—honest worth,
    That brightens more the more 'tis tried,

Will triumph yet o'er all the earth,
   And take the place of pomp and pride.
And also—the assassin's hand
   May smite the body, not the truth
That in the body bears command—
   For virtue wears immortal youth.

Montreal, Canada.

By F. L. N——.

TOLL! toll ye bells, from ev'ry belfried tower!
   Toll forth the story of the nation's woe—
From where th' Atlantic sounds the ocean's dirge
To old Pacific's shore—toll forth the knell;
Tell of the people's anguish for the dead,
The poor man's friend, the champion of the slave.
Thou, "Lord of hosts," to whom all vengeance is,
Four millions freed from slav'ry's galling chains;
The blood of hero-martyrs; send forth a prayer to Thee,
That Thou wilt hear in this our hour of need.
May we ascribe to Thee all power and might,
Praise Thee, O God! from whom all blessings flow,
And not in *man* put all that trust we owe,
To Him who holds all nations in His hands.
But may our prayer, in this dark hour of need,
When shadows thickly gather o'er our land,
Be that of Him who died that we might live.
Thy will, O God! not ours, be freely done.

By A. E. H——.

THE nation's chief is dead!
  His bright career is o'er;
To-day our bleeding country mourns,
  As she ne'er wept before!

But he's left a monument
  As deathless as his name,
Rear'd by the fiat he sent forth,
  Which broke base slavery's chain.

The solemn toll of bells
  Speaks anguish to the breast,
While booming cannon tell the tale,
  A hero's gone to rest!

The glorious stars and stripes,
  Proud emblems of our worth,
In folds of sorrow, draped in woe,
  Hang sweeping to the earth.

The strong man stands aghast,
  As the news falls on his ear;
While the deep pulsations of the heart
  Beat high with doubt and fear.

Children shall learn the tale,
  As they are taught their creed,
And execrate the monster wretch
  Who dared to do the deed!

History shall mark the page,
  The records of this crime;
While curses on the assassin's name
  Roll through all coming time.

Crowned heads shall pale with fear
  When the bloody act is told;
For the writing may be on the wall
  For them, like one of old.

The traitors of our land
  The future well may dread;
For treason's fate, in letters bold,
  Is marked on every head.

The blood of Lincoln cries
  From earthly courts to heaven,
Let justice, with her sternest power,
  To rebel heads be given.

Pray for their crimson souls,
  That grace the heart renew;
But, lest temptation overcome,
  Let the *gallows* have its due.

By EMMA.

HE sleeps, he sleeps, our noble chief,
  He rests in death's embrace;
And saddened grief is now displayed
  Upon Columbia's face;—

For her most cherished, honored son
   Has passed unto the tomb,—
A victim to a demon's plot;
   A nation mourns his doom.

Our flag—the glorious stars and stripes,
   The red, the white, and blue,
Has now another color mid
   Those bright tri-colors true.
It mourns; and hangs its sacred head,
   Baptized with many a tear,
In darkened sorrow now unfurled.
   Upon our chieftain's bier.

Like Moses on mount Pisgah's top,
   He saw the land beyond;
And in his heart he thanked God for
   The glory which had dawned.
But "death came with a lifted spear,"
   And he, the pure and true,
Was called away unto his home,
   Beyond the heaven's blue.

We trust in God, our nation's shield;
   He will His children keep,
Our "Ship of State" sails bravely on,
   And breasts the waters deep;
No hand but God's can rend our flag,
   Which floats in freedom now,
No will but His can save this land,
   And to that "Will" we bow.

Far off in future's sky, I see
   One glowing, glistening star,
It bursts, and lo, our native land
   Is free from bloody war,
Along fair Rappahannock's shore,
   There is no war-cry's ring,
But o'er each soldier's sepulchre
   There droops an angel's wing.

From the receding clouds of war,
   Appears a gleaming hand,
And holds within its tightened grasp
   The emblem of our land.
Above that hand are letters bright,
   And carved in purest gold,
"BE STILL, AND KNOW THAT I AM GOD!"
   Ye nations now behold!

By GERTRUDE.

WEEP! for a nation mourns to-day
   Her loved and honored dead.
Yea, weep! while mournful dirges play
And obsequies are said.
The father of our native land,
Our leader through this night,
Is numbered with that martyr band,
Who walk on high in white.

Just as the clouds had passed away
And dawned the morning light;

Upon *him*, dawned eternal day,
When comes no cloudy night,
Life's battles fought, its conflict o'er
There comes a peaceful calm;
His work is done, on the other shore
He waves the victor's palm.

And midst that glorious victor band,
Are those, the brave ones slain,
For freedom and their native land,
Who sleep on battle plains.
We mourn for them in cot and hall,
The loved ones fallen asleep.
Again our hearts are mourning all,
For our President, we weep.

Weep! O America, thy tears
Ne'er for more faithful fell.
In vain we glance to future years,
For one we'll love as well.
But, Christian martyr, rest in peace,
Thy faithful labors o'er;
Earth's trials, sorrows, all shall cease,
Rest, rest for evermore!

ANONYMOUS.

GONE where the angels are singing
  In the light of eternal day;
Gone where the seraphs are smiling,
  High over the starry way;

Gone where the thrones of crystal
  Gleam bright in the halls above,
Far away from earth's red passions,
  To the realms of endless love.

He may bless the hand that sent him,
  (Though a demon struck the blow)
To be free from cares woe-laden,
  In this weary land below;
Yet we cursed the fiend that robbed us
  Of the soul of his beaming eye,
And set death's darkest signet seal
  With a malice of darker dye.

The big world's breast is heaving
  With a weight that none may say;
And its eyes are cold and joyless
  As the clammy church-yard clay;
And its heart is beating sadly
  As the sound of a funeral bell,
For he was called to his resting
  While rending the chains of hell.

Gull-winged commerce, crape thy pluming;
  Turret flags fly idly now;
Sullen cannon, cease thy booming;
  Glistening furrow, spurn the plough;
For the tones that filled with gladness
  City, hamlet, valley, hill,
Now are hushed as summer twilight,
  And his lips are icy still.

River, glide through the weeping willows,
  And moan on your winding way;
For you'll miss his voice, ay, sadly,
  When your sunniest wavelets play.
Ocean, spread in trackless grandeur,
  Neath the dome of the spring-time sky
Bid your waters sigh as the night wind,
  When the rushing storm is nigh.

Thunder, growl from your airy cloud-home,
  That the nation's pride is fled;
Lightning, lance your darts in•sable,
  For man's best brother's dead;
May dews, fall in pearly beauty,
  Lightly sweet where the hero sleeps,
For he smiles from above on a mourning people,
  And o'er his country a good guard keeps.

His name will blaze in the roll of story,
  And ages coming will sigh and tell,
How he nobly fought in the cause of freedom,
  And in the cause of freedom fell.

By E. V. S———.

A NATION'S mighty heart
  Throbs with a voiceless woe;
The skies in pity weep,
  The winds are sobbing low,
The gentle stars have veiled their light,
And deep'ning gloom enshrouds the night.

The patriot heart is stilled—
  Stilled by a murderer's hand!
Strong men are bowed in grief,
  And mourning fills the land,
And countless eyes are dimmed with tears—
Sad hearts oppressed with anxious fears.

A few brief days agone
  Bells rang with merry peal:
And brightening omens told
  Our country's future weal;
Flags floated on the sun-lit air,
The night was o'er of our despair.

How changed the joyous scene!
  Now draped in midnight gloom
The stars and stripes *he* loved:—
  Oh, plant them o'er his tomb:
Thus may the sacred emblem keep
Sweet vigil o'er his peaceful sleep.

That warm and kindly heart,
  It knew no bitter thought;
With hopeful faith and love,
  Its deeds of mercy wrought:
It ne'er betrayed our fervent trust—
Our country guards the hallowed dust!

"SIC SEMPER TYRANNIS!"

ANONYMOUS.

"SIC SEMPER TYRANNIS!" Oh sentence of might,
    When pronounced in the service of freedom and
        right!
Yet how false is its meaning to true hearts and brave:
When it falls from the lips of the coward and knave.
Each drop of the blood that so basely was shed,
Like a mountain shall rest on the parricide's head;
And to those who urged on the foul fiend on his track,
"Thus ever to traitors!" we answer them back.

"Sic Semper Tyrannis!" Oh recreant State!
The words of your motto have sealed your own fate.
The blood of the bondman cried out from your soil,
The tears of his anguish, the sweat of his toil—
The right arm of justice was bared for the blow,
And the pride of the tyrant in dust is laid low;
And when the last hope of rebellion shall die,
"Thus ever with traitors!" shall sound from on high.

"Sic Semper Tyrannis!" The judgments of God
Are written in letters of blood on your sod.
Oh where was your mercy, when true hearts and brave,
By a slow wasting famine went down to the grave?
Ay, the walls of your prison a story can tell,
Which would put to the blush e'en the demons of hell;

But the arrow of justice unerring has sped,
"Thus ever with traitors!" in judgment is said.

"Sic Semper Tyrannis!" That sentence repeat,
When your hosts shall be scattered in hopeless defeat—
Nor fail to remember that you were the first
To kindle the flames of rebellion accurst.
Our protest went down from the North to the South,
Till we thundered it forth from the cannon's red mouth,
And the dust of our fathers re-echoed the cry—
"Thus ever with traitors! Ay, thus let them die!"

"Sic Semper Tyrannis!" Our life has not fled.
Though a blow has been struck at our national head,
It but adds a new impulse, and gives a fresh start,
To the true·loyal blood in the national heart;
And the future shall prove, when the conflict is done,
That the hearts of the people are beating as one,
And the words from our lips, that in judgment shall fall,
"Thus ever with traitors!" are echoed by all.

By L. H. J——.

HEARD ye that fearful knell? Its solemn tone
Proclaims the death of freedom's noblest son!
Throughout the coasts of our once favored land,
That thrilling note resounds. A traitor's hand,
Impelled by treacherous hate of all that's good,
Has dared to shed our country's dearest blood.

Heard ye that cannon's boom? It tells a tale
Of deepest woe! It is a nation's wail—
The mighty throbbings of its bitter grief
For its own chosen, honored, murdered chief.
From lake to gulf, from the Atlantic shore
To the Pacific coast, is heard its mournful roar.

Heard ye that muffled drum? It bids us pause
And weep the saddest loss to freedom's cause—
A crime that will consign the actor's name
To infamy and everlasting shame:
The foulest deed that ever sought a place
In the dark annals of the human race.

Heard ye that mournful dirge? Its plaintive strain
Fills every patriot heart with grief and pain.
It is the dirge of one that loved his race,
In whose kind heart hate never found a place;
Whose public acts were all for human good—
Who thought to favor those who shed his blood!

You sons of freemen, while you shed the tear
Of grief around your cherished chieftain's bier,
Before high Heaven resolve, that come what may,
From this sad hour until your dying day,
You will, with Heaven's aid defend "the right,"
And war for freedom with your utmost might.

Not for the freedom of a haughty few,
Who dare to claim the race for service due,
Who arrogate the right to sell and buy
Their fellow-men for hopeless slavery;

But for the freedom of the entire race—
In every clime—in every land and place.

Resolve, that from this consecrated hour,
Our country shall be free from slavery's power—
That tyranny shall die, and this shall be
Truly the glorious land of liberty—
That pride and arrogance, and savage spite,
Shall no more triumph over human right.

Resolve, that he whose death we mourn to-day,
Whose life a tyrant's minion took away,
Shall be revenged by making all men free
From the behests of blood-stained slavery—
That Lincoln—henceforth, evermore shall be
The watchword of our blood-bought liberty.

His life, the dawning of a better day;
He was the morning-star whose golden ray,
Resplendent shone upon the waning night
Amid the beams of morning's rising light.
He touched the zenith—quickly passed away
The harbinger of freedom's brighter day.

The first grand act of our great nation's play
Ends with the curtain-drop of this sad day;
To-morrow opens a new scene of things—
The joy of freemen and the grief of kings.
The nation rising from her martyr's fall,
Gives freedom and the rights of man to all!

ANONYMOUS.

DEAD! dead! struck down in his prime,
With the weight of God's mighty work on him
Dead! dead! struck down by assassins,
The tools of a cursed rebellion.
Dead in the first blush of the dawning
That breaks on the night of the ages;
On the verge of the century's triumph;
The triumph of God over Mammon.
Like Moses, he caught from his Pisgah
The wonderful glories and brightness
That glistened along the far hill-tops
Which rose o'er the land of his promise;
Like Moses, the head, heart, and spirit
Of hosts which he led on to triumph;
Like Moses he fell on the confines,
And died with the harness yet on him.

Through years of most foul persecution,
Of calumny base and black-hearted,
Dark fears, high hopes and quick perils,
War's storms, and the tempests of factions,
He steered the tos't bark of the nation.
And now, as the weary-sought haven
Just looms indistinct through the vapors;
And the breezes from landward, regaling
The sense with the perfume of olives;
And the dove, on venturous pinion,
Flies seaward to greet the returning

Of the ship that the storms and the tempests
Have wasted their strength to destroy—
Where is he, our master and pilot?
Brave heart, that unquelled and undaunted
Hath faced and defied the blasts' roaring;
Clear head, that amid all the darkness
Hath seen the far-off consummation;
Strong arm, that with grasp so unyielding
Held the helm to the hurricane's shock,
While our good ship sped on like an arrow,
Nor swerved by so much as a hand-breadth
From the path of her glory and triumph.
Dead, dead on the deck, and the nation
Stands speechless to-day! But to-morrow,
When its pulse's mighty throbbing is calmer,
And its great heart beats steady once more;
Then, better its foes had a mill-stone
About them, to drag them head downward
For aye in the depth of the ocean.
For the mill-stone's a toy and a plaything
Beside a great people's great anguish,
And the sea is a pool to the billows
Which shall roll in flood-tides of vengeance,
Deep, deep, o'er the damned assassins.
Not the two or three ruffians, the tools
In the hands of craftier masters,
For they shall escape by mere dying;
But the terrible, fierce retribution
Shall fall on the heads of the traitors
Who inspired and advised the foul murder,

So, back in the march of the centuries,
The curse fell not on the centurion;
Nor rested its weight on one Judas;
But down to the last generation,
From father to son, and to son's son,
The curse, growing heavier and heavier,
Rests, and shall rest, forever and ever.
In vain was their fiendish endeavor,
Who hoped in Christ's grave clothes and linen
To stifle man's hopes of redemption,
And bury God's will in man's tomb.
And as vain is their hope who relying
On mammon and treason and murder,
Would roll back the spring-tides of progress,
Annulling the will of Jehovah,
Consigning the world's hopes of freedom
To darkness and slavery again.

Farewell, thou, our father and brother!
The grave can receive but not hold thee;
Thy spirit shall live on triumphant;
Thy name shall be liberty's watchword;
Thy glory stream down through the ages;
Thy mem'ry be sacred to freemen;
Thy fame be thy country's and God's.

By Rev. Dr. S. D. PHELPS.

HOW is the strong staff broken,
 And rent the beauteous rod!
How strangely hast Thou spoken,
 O sovereign, righteous God!
Like startled volleyed thunder,
 Dashed from a cloudless sky,
All horror-struck, we wonder,
 And trembling ask, oh why?
Oh why this sudden sadness,
 Flung o'er our brightening path,
To fill our sky of gladness
 With awful forms of wrath?
O Father! we adore Thee:
 We know Thy reign is just;
Smitten, we bow before Thee—
 Our place is in the dust.

How is the strong staff broken!—
 The nation mourns its chief,
And showering tears betoken
 Its mighty loss and grief!
The tide of triumph swelling,
 Confounded, staggers back;
From mast and hall and dwelling,
 The banner droops in black!
Hark! freedom's bells are tolling;
 Her solemn cannons roar;

And sorrow's billows rolling,
   Break mournful on the shore.
O land! bereaved, forsaken,
   Thy head and father falls!
That life by treason taken,
   For justice loudly calls!

How is the strong staff broken,
   That held us 'mid the storm!
Our safety's cherished token,
   We clung around his form;
Till Moses-like, he renders—
   Near through the exodus—
His soul, where Nebo splendors
   Beam bright in hope for us!
Through all the strife remaining,
   Be Thou, O God, our guide,
The cause of right maintaining,
   For which our Lincoln died!
The nation's heart enshrining
   Her noblest martyr son,
Shall keep his glory shining
   Like that of Washington!

ANONYMOUS.

OUR people are mourning
   From the east to the west;
We bear to his slumber
   Our wisest and best.

A light has departed,—
  Our beacon for years,—
And left our proud nation
  In darkness and tears.

But the gloom o'er our hearts
  Will not linger long;
May those sad tears give place
  To freedom's glad song,
For our brave Lincoln's name
  Like our banner unfurled,
Will now fling its glories
  Abroad to the world.

A name to the list
  Of the names that we love,
A soul to the circle
  Of dear ones above!
A star in that banner
  The breeze never bore,
Which beams in the temple
  Of those gone before.

Oh dark was the morning
  That dawned o'er his close!
His life given up
  To the land of our foes:
In the day of our troubles
  The hope of each breast—
Our pilot in storms,
  And our haven of rest.

Our eagle will mourn
   O'er the patriot's grave,
And emblem the grief
   Of the free, and the brave,
And the couch of the sleeper
   Is holy with prayer,
And the hearts of our people
   Are gathering there.

Sad, slow was the march
   Of the funeral train,
And gloomy the banners,
   And mournful the strain;
Silent and solemn
   That multitude moved—
The homage of freedom
   To one whom they loved.

Oh thus be forever
   Our feelings outpoured,
To him who is worthy—
   The patriot's reward!
In that nation which rises
   Such men to revere,
Oh who can disunion
   Or slavery's curses fear!

By ELLERTON ROSARR.

> "Death to death by felon hand
> For guarding well his fatherland."

WEEP for the nation's sins, heap ashes on the head;
    And humbly bend in fervent prayer,
Like the holy man that's dead.

Let the nation's tears o'erflow, and with muffled footsteps tread,
As they look on the face of the uncrowned king;
The mighty man that's dead.

The uplifting of his hand, last night the nation led;
Cursed be the traitor heart, and hand,
Who smote the mighty dead.

The great men of our Senate-house, with grief bow down the head,
And the soldier mourns, and the poor man weeps
For the great true heart, that's dead.

The negro lifts free hands to Heaven, who erst in chains was led,
And blesses the God who made us all
For the mighty man that's dead.

  Montreal, Canada.

By MARTHA PERRY LOWE.

LAY him to rest; lay him deep in the ground;
Full long enough ye have borne him around,
With the tramping of horses, the weary drum beat,
Before all the eyes, and the glare of the street:—
    Lay him to rest.

They were eyes full of love, they were eyes that did
  weep,
And the chillness of death on the cities did creep;
But now let him go, gentle friends, to his rest;
Let him go to his home in the heart of the West:—
    Lay him to rest.

Why did we take him from fair Illinois?
He was young in her woods, he was fresh as a boy:—
Why did we set him in that high place,
And bring all the furrows of care to his face?

Why do we send him back to his land,
With a blood mark upon him from traitorous hand?
Why do we show them the wound in his head,
And say not a word but "behold he is dead?"

We brought him from westward because he was just;
We made him our chieftain, we gave him our trust;
Serene in the midst of the tumult he stood,
And we learned that 'tis greatest of all to be good.

We've let him die for us—yes, we've let him die,
With his armor all on, as the soldier boys lie;

Not a moment of warning—a message to tell;
And we say he sleeps well—and we say he sleeps well!

Be proud, Illinois, for to you it was given
To raise up the noblest of martyrs for heaven!
Be pure, Illinois, for now 'tis your part
To let the dear ashes repose on your heart!
   Lay him to rest, lay him to rest
    On Illinois' breast!

By G. F. S——.

O THOU, whose voice from Sinai's mount
 In tones of thunder spake,
While lightnings girt her summit round,
 And made the mountain quake;
Whose ways mysterious, mandates just,
 In wondrous power displayed,
Doth lay whole nations in the dust,
 And strike their rulers dead—

Hear Thou our supplicating prayer,
 "And when Thou hearest forgive;"
O Lord! our bleeding country spare,
 And bid our Union live.
Our land in human blood is steeped
 By fratricidal war;
While "Rachel for her children weeps,"
 We mourn our second sire.

Not blood of bulls nor goats is sent
   For sin our sacrifice,
But our beloved PRESIDENT
   On freedom's altar dies!
O Lord! in mercy, not in wrath,
   Make known to us Thy will,
Guide us by love in wisdom's path,
   And say Thou, "PEACE, be still."

By Mrs. J. T. ROBINSON.

"BE still—and know that I am God!"
   Father, to this sublime decree,
We, smarting 'neath Thy fearful rod,
   Adore the grace we cannot see.

We trusted that our honor'd head
   Would bring us to the promised land,
But Thou to Pisgah's top hast led,
   Pointed—and then withdrew Thy hand.

It was a fiend who did the deed
   Which turned a nation's joy to woe;
But He who knows a nation's need,
   Will thro' that wrath His praises show.

God is not dead. He rules the wave;
   Our Ship of State shall not go down;
Jesus but sleeps—He'll wake to save,
   And tyrant storms shall feel His frown.

But oh! our loved, our lost, our true!
    Our country's saviour, hope and stay!
Murdered and martyred saint! for you
    We weep in bitterness to-day.

Father! forgive not his high crime
    Who aimed at Christ in killing him,
Bring to a punishment condign,
    The wretch, who did the murderous sin.

ANONYMOUS.

"Only the actions of the just
Smell sweet and blossom in the dust."

O FATHERLAND! the homesteads of whose sires
  Are smoking still with sacrificial fires,
    Whose offerings alone—
Thy choicest children, beautiful and brave—
    For wrong could not atone:

O land! upon whose scarred and bleeding breast
Thy countless heroes lie, securely pressed,
    Out of the wrath of sin,
Open once more its all-enshrouding vest,
    And fold your best beloved in!

And let us weep that one with faith so great,
Whose peerless patience thus could watch and wait
    To work the great release,
Thus, only, stricken from his high estate,
    Might enter into peace.

And, bringing laurel for the good man's grave,
Blest in the heritage he died to save,
  Let all the people come,
And vow its future worthily shall wear
  This crowning martyrdom.

And on and on, through all the circling years,
Humanity shall tend the sod with tears,
  Till from its greatness grows
That tree of righteousness, in whose broad shade
  The nations shall repose.

By JENNIE E. S——

MOURN all in fair Columbia's land,
  Lament, with grief complain,
Our President so dear to all,
  By traitor's hands is slain.
How much we loved and honored him,
  We only now discover,
Both North and South have lost a friend,
  Who loved them as a brother.

Oh! with what joy we did receive,
  The news of Lee's surrender;
We fired guns, and banners raised,
  To tell of victory's splendor.
Alas! we did not know that grief
  Was soon to mar our gladness,
And every heart that throbbed with joy,
  Throbs now in gloom and sadness.

These sable hangings everywhere,
   Speak of the inward sorrow
That lies within each loyal heart;
   None need feel grief or sorrow.
We ill could spare our hero brave,
   In such a time of trouble;
We ill could spare him any time,
   Which makes our sorrow double.

Oh! cursed be he whose murderous heart
   Was by black treason stirred,
And aimed so sure that fatal shot;
   Would God that it had erred.
But God, whose ways mysterious are,
   Removed our chosen one;
Then let the nation, while it mourns,
   Say Lord, Thy will be done.

Then lay our patriot down to rest;
   To sleep that dreamless slumber;
And may his spirit mild be found
   Among the chosen number.
We'll mourn for him, our martyred one,
   Our bells toll mournful strains,
And e'en the clouds, that float above,
   Drop tears in gentle rains.

Rest, LINCOLN, rest, thy well-run course
   With honor thou hast ended;
None ever served his country more,
   Or more her rights defended.

Rest, hero brave, thy noble deeds
  Will live through many ages;
Thine honored name fill many a place,
  In coming history's pages.

By P. G. FAIRFIELD.

THE curtains of the midnight darkly fell
  O'er that fair city by Potomac's side;
And low the April wind with ebb and swell
  Of mournful pinions swept the classic tide.

While erst our heroes stood in serried arms—
  Where senate's fathers high in council sate,
So late the scene of war and dread alarms,
  Again o'ershadowed with a nation's fate.

Scarce had the meek-eyed dove of peace and hope
  Its happy pinions over fields outspread,
Where gory-handed war in vale and slope
  Impaled the victims to his altar led.

And scarce her golden wings had new-born love
  Spread like a smile of God upon the land
Where' brother against brother deadly strove
  On many a field with fratricidal hand,

When the assassin's bullet sought the brain
  Of him whose arm a nation's law upheld!
The blow was struck, as lightning rives in twain
  The forest-king by thunder-tempest felled.

Columbia's genius, guardian of the land,
    Ah, why was thy protecting ægis furled?—
Nor interposed to turn aside the hand
    Which earned the execration of the world!

Not as the warrior falls on gory fields,
    With glory wrapped about him as a shroud;
Not as the peaceful man his spirit yields,
    Or he whose hoary form with age is bowed,

He fell. A nation's highest magistrate,
    In whose high oath a people's mandate spoke;
By rash assassination met his fate,
    Riven as lightning rives the stately oak.

Then let the nation weep; and draped in weeds
    Be trailed that banner erst in war unfurled,
Which borne by heroes earned immortal meeds,
    And won the plaudits of a wondering world!

Let toil lay by his hammer; not a sound
    Disturb the stillness of a people's grief,
For him who fell, fell by the coward's wound,
    As thieving autumn kills the summer leaf.

For it is meet we pause amid this show
    Of pomp and triumph—pause to drop a tear
O'er him who fell, the patriot laid low
    In death upon a nation's storied bier.

By J. McL——.

YES; he is coming home!
O prairie-land, his own land of the West!
Open thine arms and fold him to thy breast,
And blossom into flowers above his place of rest!

Four years ago, amid the stormy night,
 Thou gavest him to be our chosen guide;
 Now that the winds and waves in peace subside,
And, with the dawn, the eastern sky is bright.

He comes! he comes! his life's great labor done,
 Among the friends and scenes he loved to sleep!
 O mourning people, wherefore should ye weep?
Is not his fame complete, his victory won?

Could years have added lustre to his name,
 Who, through the perils of the darkest hour,
 With such rare wisdom held the reins of power,
Alike unspoiled by praise, unmoved by blame?

Or set in purer light the blameless life,
 The heart of more than woman's tenderness,
 So ready to forgive, so quick to bless;
So bravely gentle 'midst the fiercest strife?

His faith, firm fixed in Him who rules on high,
 Sublimely patient through the storm he stood;
 Then sealed his life's devotion with his blood,
And found his recompense beyond the sky!

O mighty West, we give him back to thee,
   Death-crowned and glorious! On his quiet brow,
   The martyr's coronet is gleaming now,
Could we but check those blinding tears to see.

In vain, in vain! As through the mourning land,
   In solemn state the grand procession sweeps,
   We only feel our friend, our father sleeps,
And we have lost his guiding voice and hand.

To other men and other days be left
   The task to weigh, to measure, and approve
   The noble heart that won a nation's love,
And, passing, leaves us orphaned and bereft.

For us—whose tears fall like the summer rain—
   Be this the tribute to his memory given,
   To keep the vow we register in heaven,
"*Our martyred dead shall not have died in vain.*"

By C. P. CRANCH.

BUT yesterday—the exulting nation's shout
   Swelled on the breeze of victory through our streets,
But yesterday—our banners flaunted out
   Like flowers the south wind woos from their retreats:
Flowers of the nation, blue, and white, and red,
   Waving from balcony, and spire, and mast;
Which told us that war's wintry storm had fled,
   And spring was more than spring to us at last.

To-day—the nation's heart lies crushed and weak;
   Drooping and draped in black our banners stand.
Too stunned to cry revenge, we scarce may speak
   The grief that chokes all utterance through the land.
God is in all. With tears our eyes are dim,
Yet strive through darkness to look to Him!

No, not in vain he died—not all in vain,
   Our good, great President! This people's hands
Are linked together in one mighty chain
   Drawn tighter still in triple-woven bands
To crush the fiends in human masks, whose might
   We suffer, oh too long! No league, nor truce
Save men with men! The devils we must fight
   With fire! God wills it in this deed. This use
We draw from the most impious murder done
   Since Calvary. Rise then, O countrymen!
Scatter these marsh-light hopes of Union won
   Through pardoning clemency. Strike, strike again!
Draw closer round the foe a girdling flame.
We are stabbed whene'er we spare—strike in God's
   name!

By Mrs. C. M. STEBBINS.

HARK, 'tis a wail of sadness!
   That stirs the loyal soul;
The bells that ring with gladness,
   Send forth a solemn toll.

The nation's chief has fallen—
   Struck by a traitor's hand—

The stars and stripes upholding,
  The noblest of the land.

Upon his country's altar
  He laid the sacrifice;
A life so pure and holy
  Hath earned a heavenly prize.

Our bleeding country's laurels
  He snatched from lawless hand,
That shall in future story
  A nation's beacon stand.

Slain on proud freedom's altar,
  To set the bondman free,
And bring to Afric's daughters,
  The year of jubilee.

A nation's heart enshrines thee,
  Best and noblest of our race,
And white-robed throngs in heaven
  Wait to welcome and embrace.

ANONYMOUS.

WHENCE comes that thrilling undertone of woe,
  That wail of sorrow, heard from high and low?
Why do strong men stand trembling with affright,
As though some awful darkness ruled the night?
Oh! why do parted lips refuse to speak,
While the pale face and boding gestures break
Tidings of evil to the startled eye?

At length—O heart, grow still!—we hear the cry,
"He whom we trusted for our nation's guide,
Is basely murdered in his manhood's pride!"
While yet glad shouts of vict'ry fill the air,
And our worn hearts still breathe the grateful prayer
Of deep thanksgiving for such blessings sent
In quick succession, till the tidings blent
In one full chorus of o'erwhelming joy.
Men crowd to hear: moved by one impulse now,
Before their Maker rev'rently they bow,
And give to Him the homage of their praise,
And seek His guidance through the future days.
How gentle peace diffused her healing art,
And breathed forgiveness in each melted heart!
Our recent foes were brethren; we would show
Compassion for their self-inflicted woe,
Would be the first our confidence to prove,
In their returning wisdom, if not love.

How could we then in this triumphant hour,
Dream that conspiracy, in lurking power,
Was seeking to destroy our nation's life,
And rouse again a fiercer, deadlier strife?
How could we think that pale-faced murder stood
Ready to strike the tried, the wise, the good,—
All whose firm hands in this eventful hour
Could guide our counsels by their well-known power?
These names struck from the roll of living men,
The dark-eyed plotters deemed that once again
War and misrule might triumph on our soil,
And make a mock'ry of our foregone toil.

But ah! God rules above. He knows full well
Each brooding counsel and each purpose fell.
The many shall not fall, but why, oh why
Must our loved chief a martyred victim lie,
With the calm smile of rest upon his brow,
Unconscious of the crowds, who, weeping, bow
In swelling anguish o'er the well-known face,
As though its features they would sadly trace
Upon their inmost souls? Unconscious, too,
How, when swift-winged the evil tidings flew,
But one deep wail broke from the nation's heart,
In which even prattling infancy took part,
And in its tiny badges of distress,
Sought earnestly its sorrow to confess;
From every home, sad draperies of woe
Reveal the grief the suffering inmates know;
In every church through all the weeping land,
What crowds of mourners at God's altar stand,
And 'neath the sable emblems of our grief,
Pay a last tribute to our fallen chief?
When 'mid the nations was it known before,
That one sad funeral reached from shore to shore?

For days the pulse of commerce faintly beats,
While saddened footsteps echo through our streets.
'Tis not alone that one so good and brave
Is thus, untimely, hurried to the grave.
'Tis not alone that he, the people's choice,
And called to office by the people's voice,
Should be removed by Heaven's all-wise decree,
Just when his heart was cheered by victory.

It is that crime should riot in the land;
That we in trembling impotence should stand
In the assassin's power; that our proud name
Must thus be linked with infamy and shame;
That we, who boast obedience to the laws,
Should know such traitors to the common cause.
It is that we, who fondly hoped to trust,
Have in these deep-laid plottings learned distrust
Of once-named, once-loved brothers. O! our God,
Whose only Son these paths of suff'ring trod,
Who knows our every thought, feels every woe,
Oh! look in mercy on Thy people now,
And hold our hearts from sin! Oh, let the right
O'er all our land prevail! Let men serve Thee,
And in that service learn true liberty!

Father! what Thou wouldst teach we fain would learn;
Unto Thy throne with humbled hearts we turn.
Oh! guide us, Father, in Thine own wise way!
Let not our footsteps from Thy precepts stray!
A child among the nations, let us prove
Thine, Father, in obedience and love.
Oh! bind us once again in strength and power,
United still in dark misfortune's hour;
United when prosperity shall shine
On happy homes, poured by Thy hand divine!
Thy blessing on our land we humbly seek!
The burden of our souls we cannot speak!
But Thou, who seest each inborn thought arise,
Oh, answer from Thy dwelling in the skies!

Hist'ry repeats how nations prouder far
Than we, and proudly versed in arts of war,
Have lost the glory of their ancient name,
And hold no semblance of their former fame.
They too forgot Thee, or they knew Thee not,
And Thou by us, alas, hast been forgot.
Oh! lead us then in penitence to bow,
And render Thee our fervent worship now.
Inspire our nation's counsels. Let them prove
A bond of union and a tie of love;
And thus dependent on Thy holy will,
Oh let us seek Christ's mission to fulfill,—
Carry the light of truth from clime to clime,
Till every nation own Thy power divine,
And in the tribute of their praises bring
Glory to God, their Saviour and their King!

By ANGELINE R. DEMBY.

WE mourn, to learn that we are struck
    With such appalling wo;
We bow beneath the mighty stroke;
    'Twas God who willed it so.

A martyr to sweet freedom's laws,
    A patriot true and brave,
With noble brow and form erect,
    Is stricken to the grave.

The grave shall not environ him;
    His spirit is with God;

It took its flight at early morn,
  When Jesus spoke the word.

"Come unto me, beloved son,
  You filled your place of trust;
I call you hence, come unto me;
  I'll raise you from the dust."

The nation mourns a patriot slain!
  Lord, heal the broken heart.
We cannot bear this stunning pain,
  Unless Thou heal the smart.

Thy balm apply to bleeding hearts;
  Our comfort Thou shalt be.
It was Thy will that we should part
  With him who made us free.

In bondage dark, oppressed with shame,
  We long were made to stand,
Till Abraham Lincoln did proclaim
  Freedom throughout the land.

God bless the true republican!
  His name shall ever live,
Till God shall unto every man
  Perpetual freedom give.

Though we still weep, we will not stand,
  With folded hands and mourn—
But, with all friends of Abraham,
  We'll trample treason down.

TO MRS. LINCOLN.

By MARY A. DENNISON.

IF it be any joy to know
That a whole nation mourns thy woe;
That clasped hands and bowed down head
Bear witness for the mighty dead;
That he was loved as ne'er before
A chief in peace or chief in war;
Take this one drop of balm—and less
By that thy draught of bitterness!

If it be any joy to feel
That thine is now the nation's weal;
That every home would gladly be
A shelter, and a shrine for thee;
That every heart throbs high to make
Some sacrifice for his dear sake:
Take this one thought of comfort,—less
May be thy draught of bitterness.

If it be any joy to see
One glimpse of thy high destiny,
As she who wore a martyr's love—
And wears an angel's now, above—
As she who felt the throbs that swelled
That heart, by hearts of millions knelled:
Take this sweet sympathy—and less
By that thy draught of bitterness!

Oh! wife of our dear patriot—see—
Our land sheds tear for tear with thee;
Yet, widow of the nation! God
Speaks to thee, through the broken sod;
"I am thy God— thou yet shall see
It was not death, but victory!
And even now my love shall bless
And drain thy cup of bitterness."

By MARY E. HART.

WATCHED ye the dawn of the still Sabbath morning?
Saw ye the sunbeams creep over the hills?
Valleys and meadows and mountains adorning,
    Waking to beauty each streamlet and rill?

Felt ye the hush that attended its coming?
    Marked ye the stillness from hillside to shore?
Still, through the silence the cannon's deep booming
    Broke on the ear with its heavy, deep roar.

While yet its echoes were ling'ring and dying,
    Heard ye, as through the still morning they rolled,
Speaking to voices from hill-tops replying,
    Sounds of the bells which so heavily tolled.

Booming and tolling in mournful succession,
    Heard ye their music with awe and surprise?

Watched ye the star-spangled banner uprisen,
  Swinging half-masted in black draperies?

Caught ye their language, this still Sabbath morning,
  Know ye the story they fluttered and told?
Spoke they of victory's glorious dawning,
  Followed by death damps terrific and cold?

Linked and united in booming and tolling,
  Mingled and twining in banners and crape—
This was the speech that was flapping and rolling,
  "Lincoln lies dead—let a mourning land weep."

Heavily fell the first news of his death-blow,
  Mutely we looked at each other in grief—
Speechless we bowed 'neath this terrible sorrow,
  Then rent the heavens with a cry for relief.

Spoke we, "God help us, what shall we be doing,"
  Prayers burst from lips that before had not prayed,
Eyes which to tears were a stranger were flowing,
  The people all mourn, for Lincoln was dead.

Who can save us, but He who from heaven
  Looked on the murderer, and gave him His will?
Which of us all shall tell why He has given
  Power to a foeman to work us this ill?

Short-sighted all, we can trace but His working,
  As the days bring us the tidings they bear;
Bowing with reverence when tempests are breaking,
  Waiting in patience till clouds disappear.

Then we shall know all the meanings of sorrow,
    Filling the air on this fair Sabbath day;
Trust we the while, in the hope that the morrow
    Find us with darkness and doubt cleared away.

By B. S. PARKER.

THE voice is hushed, the heart is still,
    The lids inclose the earnest eyes,
That only wake for Zion's hill,
    And only beam for Paradise.

We kindle brightly to thy praise,
    We melt in sorrow at thy bier,
And wonder in the boundless days,
    When God shall every truth insphere,

In sinless orbits of delight
    What crowns thy spirit brow shall wear,
When part the terror and the night,
    Thou soarest into morning there.

Oh choral lips of love and song;
    The world's harmonic multitude—
That through the ages dim and long,
    Have prophesied the coming good.

Philosopher and saint and seer
    Of every age and race and clime,
Behold the promised days are near,
    Auroral on the hills of time!

We read the blessed morrow's sign
   That comes to hallow every place,
In every feature, every line
   Of that upturned and calmest face.

From this dear sacrifice we learn
   The future's full reality,
How freedom's flame shall mount and burn
   Above the tomb of slavery.

How age on age shall pile its weight,
   Yet through the twilight dim and far,
Among the wise and good and great,
   Shall Lincoln shine a morning star.

The useless lash, the broken chain,
   Black swarms of traffic turned to men,
War fruiting with eternal gain,
   That ripens into peace again.

These glorify the places where
   Thy paths have been, O true and brave!
And melodize the western air,
   To sing of rest above thy grave.

Rest, patriot-martyr, saviour, friend,
   Defender of the poor and weak!
Thy glory shall not have an end
   While history has a voice to speak.

In deathless harmonies of song,
   In Alpine heights of eloquence,

Where hearts are tender, love is strong,
  Shall live thy sweet beneficence,

And breathe its blessings evermore
  Through all the scope of coming years,
While thou on freedom's wings shall soar
  In love's celestial atmospheres.

In love's celestial atmospheres
  That musical shall ever be
With this—that charms immortal ears—
  "Through Christ the Lord, he made men free."

By E. J. W——.

TOLL the bells throughout the country
  With a solemn, tender peal;
Bow each head with bitter sorrow,
  Round the altar lowly kneel.

Toll the bells: they'll not awake him
  From his slumber calm and deep;
Toll the bells throughout the country
  As our mighty nation weeps:

Weeps for him, the friend of freedom,
  He who made the bondman free;—
Long as earth endures, shall glory
  Shine o'er his blest memory.

Raise each heart and voice to Heaven,
  Remorse upon the murd'rer prey!

While the nation weeps in anguish
    Him who lies so still to-day.

Toll the bells;—his form was noble,—
    Never shall we see it more;
Weep, lament for him passed from us
    Out upon the shining shore.

Full of health and strength when ushered
    Into life beyond the stream
That is swelling all around us,
    Ere we catch a distant gleam.

Little did we think a Judas,
    Foul Iscariot was near,
And that when our hearts were joyful,
    Close by joy there stood a bier.

From Thy throne in heaven, O Father,
    Hear us as we humbly pray,
That Thou'lt raise us up another
    Like the one just passed away.

Wilt Thou not in vengeance visit
    The foul Judas with Thy wrath?
Evermore let sorrow bind him,
    Never more joy cross his path.

Toll the bells for him who lieth
    Still and cold in death's embrace;
Weep, lament for him passed from us,
    Is there one to take his place?

Toll the bells with solemn pealing,
   Through our loved and native land,
And as through the air they echo,
   May we all united stand.

ANONYMOUS.

GREAT men will speak and write thy praise,
   Through untold ages yet to come.
The good in every land will raise
   The voice of mourning o'er thy doom.

For thee a nation mourns to-day:
   The sounds of mirth and joy are still.
A traitor's blow has dealt dismay,
   And caused a nation's blood to chill.

Thine with Washington's great name
   "On history's storied page will shine,"
Of martyrs with undying fame
   In ages past, the brightest thine.

Of thine—no glaring fault or deed
   Has tinged the country's cheek with shame;
God sent thee in her time of need,
   To rule with high and holy aim.

We tremble for our country's fate,
   With thy controlling wisdom gone.
No guides-man of our "Ship of State,"
   Than thee, has richer laurels won.

By JOSEPHINE WHITE.

COLUMBIA mourns in bitterest woe,
    Above a martyr's blood-stained bier;
Grief's sable garb enshrouds her now,
    She sees her children bathed in tears.
Go! look! o'er all her wide domains,
    Her mountains, plains, and villages fair,
Where, late ten thousand banners waved,
    While shouts of victory rent the air.

Ay look! and see, no banners now,
    Forth on the breeze in triumph flow,
But sadly droop, their bright folds draped
    With emblems of a nation's woe;
And victory weeping, points where flow
    Our martyred hero's precious blood,
While peace, her white wings stained with gore,
    Lies prostrate by the crimson flood.

Well may we weep: our brightest star
    Is gone! its lustre quenched in woe,
We mourn our martyred Lincoln now,
    By coward hands in death laid low;
Ay! murderous hands have done the deed,
    That even fiends would blush to name,
A deed which thrills the heart with dread,
    And fills the meanest soul with shame.

Ah! let our tears in torrents flow,
    And let us mourn our noble dead,

Drape all our land in weeds of woe,
  Our Lincoln's mighty soul has fled;
His hand gave freedom! blessed boon,
  He laid the power of tyrants low,
He forged no chain to bind the weak,
  He triumphed o'er no conquered foe.

Lincoln has fallen! yet he lives,
  Enshrined within each noble soul!
His name! Columbia's pride shall be,
  As countless ages o'er her roll;
It need not be with matchless skill,
  Carved on the towering marble fair,
Go look upon each patriot's heart,
  Behold! 'tis deeply graven there.

And though we mourn we say with pride,
  He gave his life in freedom's cause,
His precious blood was barely shed,
  Defending our most sacred laws;
And not while blessed freedom lives,
  Be peace or war our country's lot,
While we can claim this land our own,
  Be Lincoln's name or deed forgot.

By BELLE F——.

BUT later from town and village
  A joyous pæan rose,
And many a voice caught up the strain,
  "We're vanquishing our foes!"

A key-note 'twas of Liberty,
　Of Freedom near at hand,
And every patriot heart was thrilled
　Throughout our storm-tossed land.

Then glad hearts flung our banner out
　To float upon the breeze;
And brighter seemed each star and stripe,
　Waving o'er land and seas.

The olive branch began to twine
　Around the deadly spear,
And Hope sang out in bugle notes
　"Redemption draweth near!"

Alas, alas, for human hopes!
　A breath—a word—a blow—
And hearts but yesterday elate,
　To-day are plunged in woe.

A nation's songs to dirges turn;
　Our banners sables wear;
And every loyal heart is touched,
　For *all* the sorrows share.

All, all, who love the truth and right,
　Who love humanity,
Who ever mourn when good men die,
　Must mourn for such as he.

We need not name the man, whose deeds
　Each loyal heart has thrilled;

And none but traitors fail to mourn
  A heart so noble, stilled.

O God! 'tis hard to feel *Thy* hand
  Hath dealt this heavy blow;
Yet Thou art at the helm, and safe
  Our bark will onward go.

Thou'st led our ship through many a storm,
  Through many a bloody sea;
It strikes a rock to-day, O God!
  And none can help, save Thee.

By SHIRLEY.

THE glories of our birth and state
  Are shadows, not substantial things;
There is no armor against fate;
  Death lays his icy hand on kings;
    Sceptre and crown
    Must tumble down,
And in the dust be equal made
With the poor crooked scythe and spade.

Some men with swords may reach the field,
  And plant fresh laurels where they kill;
But their strong nerves at length must yield:
  They fame but one another still!
    Early or late
    They stoop to fate,

And must give up their murmuring breath,
When they, pale captives, creep to death.

The garlands wither on your brow—
  Then boast no more your mighty deeds;
Upon Death's purple altar, now,
  See where the victor victim bleeds.
      All hands must come
      To the cold tomb—
Only the actions of the just
Smell sweet and blossom in the dust.

By MARY ROBBINS.

ABRAHAM LINCOLN! here we stand,
  North and South and East and West,
Round thy coffin, hand in hand;
  Hear us from thy place of rest!
    Abraham Lincoln, freedom's martyr,
    Here we swear we will not falter
  In the cause thou lovedst best.

By the graves at Gettysburg
  Thou thyself didst consecrate
Unto Jesus; now the land
  Mourns thine own untimely fate.
    Abraham Lincoln, Christian martyr,
    By thy grave as by an altar,
  We ourselves do consecrate.

To a firmer trust in God,
  To a kindlier faith in man;
Sharing even the heaviest load
    If we may help save our land.
        Abraham Lincoln, patriot, martyr,
        Thou didst never faint nor falter;
    May we worthy of thee stand!

Praying, fighting for the right,
  Till foul treason's bloody hand
Fades away in endless night
    From our glad enfranchised land.
        Oh, our great Emancipator!
        Thanks of true men, curse of traitor,
    Cannot reach where thou dost stand.

Weeping o'er thy grave we bend,
  Freedmen, freemen, one in grief;
Even the South has lost a friend,
    And the traitor's joy is brief:
        For we swear, oh murdered martyr!
        We'll to treason give no quarter,
    As we rally round our chief.

By E. V. R——.

WITH earnest heart, unshrinkingly upholding
  The awful cause God raised him to protect;
With patient heart, the mighty scheme unfolding,
  Looking to Him to counsel and direct.

Steadfast and calm, through hopes deferred, defeated;
    Saddened by many cares, oppressed by none;
Thank God! he lived to see that work completed,
    Then passed away from earth—his work was done.

Done! Not so it seemeth to our darkened vision;
    Still do the shadows veil the dawning light;
But hope like his failed never of fruition,
    Since God is on the throne, and judgeth right.

Pure, humble heart, unstained by selfish quarrel,
    Amid the strife of party ever calm,
He gladly twined our heroes' brows with laurel,
    Then bowed his own to wear the martyr's palm.

Kind, tender heart, through all its pulses thrilling
    With pity for a captive brother's woe;
No rest for him, while steadfastly fulfilling
    God's solemn mandate, "Let my people go."

No rest for him, who felt each slave's oppression,
    Who knew their blood for blood must loudly call;
No rest till he effaced the foul transgression;
    Then gave his own, the dearest blood of all.

And now, around his bier a weeping nation
    Their ardent love and gratitude express:
Not with a mournful dirge of lamentation,
    But with a solemn, thrilling tenderness.

His was the courage and the strength that bore them
    Through the lone wilderness and sea of blood:

Who, when the promised land stretched fair before them,
    Upon the towering summit meekly stood;

Saw them, ere long, that peaceful land possessing,
    Above all nations prosperous and blest,—
Then, lifting up his voice in solemn blessing,
    He passed unto his everlasting rest.

And on each heart his words of benediction,
    With sad, prophetic meaning, now must fall:
"Patience and faith in every dark affliction;
    Malice to none, but charity to all."

Mourn then, but not for him—he died victorious;
    A memory more cherished none could crave;
God took his spirit to a rest most glorious,
    We lay his body in an honored grave.

By S. J. D———.

THE crowning act of treason's done,
    America now mourns her son;—
        Her noblest and her best.

Struck by the assassin's dastard hand,
Who would have thought our favor'd land
        Would shelter such a fiend?

Each heart is filled with gloom and woe,
And bitter tears our eyes o'erflow,
        For one so loved and dear.

Forever hushed that kindly voice,
Whose virtues made him twice the choice
  Of every loyal heart.

Ay, drape the flag, and drape each home,
Another heart may never come
  So purely true as his.

The olive branch was budding fast,
But now the day of peace is past,
  The nursing hand is gone.

The country bleeds at every pore,
For him who'll guide our ship no more
  Through angry storm and rain.

A nation's heart is bowed in grief,
Her outraged feelings find relief
  Alone in justice done.

Mercy will fold her wing and flee,
Avenging justice now will be,
  Our watchword and our song.

We knew that thou wert always dear,
And memory'll keep thee very near
  Unto our loving hearts.

But, oh! we knew not love so strong,
Could to the human heart belong,
  As that which weeps for thee!

Within thy cold and narrow bed,
Thy sleep is sweet. Thou art not dead,
    Thy voice shall still be heard.

Children will bless thee in their prayer;
Thy mem'ry 'll linger on the air,
    For ages yet to come.

Fearless of death, thou didst not dream,
A soul was born that had no gleam
    Of human feeling left.

But thou art gone, and we are left,
Of thy kind, tender care bereft,
    Our mighty loss to feel.

We see thy form all stiff and cold,
Now ready for the earth and mould,
    But thou art with thy God.

Thy days of weariness are o'er,
Thy feet we trust now tread the shore
    Of that eternal life,

Where wars ne'er come or jarring strife,
To mar the sweetness of thy life,
    That ends no more.

By CARRIE.

LET him rest, his work is o'er,
Nor from the celestial shore
Recall ye him.
In death he sleeps!
    Toll, O bell,
      A solemn knell—
A nation weeps.

Hark! even now a nation's moan,
Rising still with anguished tone,
Comes on the breeze.
Let the tears flow!
    Toll, O bell,
      A solemn knell,
He lieth low.

Stricken by a traitor hand,
Let it bear the deepest brand
Of infamy.
Still! heart be still!
    Cannon, boom!
      Sound treason's doom
From vale and hill.

Close the eyes whose light has fled,
Bear him now with muffled tread
To his last rest.

Bow low the head!
    Shine out ye stars—
    Droop down ye bars
O'er our loved dead.

Cease to fall, O bitter tears;
Through the veil of future years
See his uprising.
Cover all hate!
    So bells toll—
    Ye drums roll—
In patience wait.

For when by the martyr grave,
Awaits "He who died to save,"
His voice shall call.
Stifle each step!
    O bells, cease—
    Rest in peace—
He lives on high.

Sacred ever to his name—
Graven on the scroll of fame
For all time.
Shrined in our love!
    Nor bell toll—
    For his soul
Reigneth above.

GONE.

ANONYMOUS.

AH, no more, like ancient Israel,
    Shall a loving nation say,
"We have Abraham for our father,"
    Lord, be with us in this day!

Gone the hand that would have moulded
    All the fragments in accord,
And from shattered blocks rebuilded
    The temple of our Lord!

Under this vast sorrow's shadow
    All our glory seems but dross,
As we gaze at one another
    With an awful sense of loss.

When creation in perfection
    Lay before its Maker's gaze,
He but called it "good," as holding
    That the highest, truest praise.

Thus from faltering lips and voices
    Our sad cry goes up this day,
Not, "how are the mighty fallen,"
    But—"the good has passed away."

MEMORY OF ABRAHAM LINCOLN.

By BEN. J. RADFORD.

HE loosed the captive's bands, and millions from
The dust sprang up and saw the light; he called,
And answering to that call the sable forms
Filled up the ranks of war to do and die
For Liberty, scarce tasted, but so sweet.
And then, for lack of wisdom, sons of men
Cried out with fear and trembling:
"Abraham Lincoln! beware of the day
When the 'poor, blind Samson' shall march to the fray!
You preside in the temple, on Liberty's throne—
Oh! let not the slave touch its pillars of stone;
And if you would free the blind wretch from his chain
Oh! send him away to his kindred again;
But bring him not here in his terrible might
Where our idols are placed and our altars burn bright.
You would bring him, unshorn, from the dungeon and grate,
To serve in the temple where myriads wait,
And, freed by his blindness, from prudent alarms,
Its pillars resign to his sinewy arms.
'Tis the story of old: the iconoclast bends
In his might, and the wail of the dying ascends—
The ruins have equalled the ruler and slave—
The worshipped and worshipper sleep in one grave.
Abraham Lincoln! 'tis time to forbear,
In the name of the goddess we pray you beware;
For the nations are gathering the temple about
To see this blind Samson, and join in the shout

When the fall shall destroy the altar and hearth,
Leaving bondage to millions and darkness to earth;
If the vile hands of traitors our altars profane
We pledge you our heart's blood to wipe out the stain;
And if they have trampled our forefathers' graves,
Give not the sweet morsel of vengeance to slaves.
We will serve in the temple and bow at the throne,
But let not the slave touch the pillars of stone."

But he in patience still possessed his soul,
And waited for the proof, and even as
The people said, the poor blind Samson pulled the
Temple down, and crushed beneath "the choice
Nobility and flower," immingled with
The gods and altars they had reared; but lo,
Our temple stands—they were the Philistines.
Within that other temple, still enthroned,
The goddess sits, but weeping now, and clad
In the habiliments of woe for him,
Her martyred son, who first gave freedom to
The slave, then gave him war to teach him what
It cost, and something of its worth.

By WINIFRED ST. CLAIR.

BRUSH aside the golden curtain
  Of the starry beaming night,
Or the flushed and tinted mantle
  Of the early morning light,

Or the long and melting shadows
    Of the morn's soft silvered ray,
As it glints the distant waters
    Turning midnight into day.
In the richest crystal chalice
    Pure and sparkling waters pour,
From the tow'ring cloud capp'd mountains,
    And the thundering ocean's roar—
Gem the chalice rich and glowing,
    With the fairest flowers that grow,
Rare and white, and blooming brightly
    Purer than the brooklets flow.
Brush aside the golden curtain,
    Here beneath the evening sky,
List ye to the blended music
    As it fills the air on high,
As it hovers o'er the resting
    Of our chieftain brave and true,
And it hymns a nation's mourning
    As it floats the ether blue.
Music sweet and holy,
    That soothes the troubled soul,
That calms life's tossing billows,
    In their madd'ning roll.
That calms life's tossing billows,
    That soothes the aching heart,
As one by one the loved and dear
    From life's pathway depart.
Brush aside the rosy curtain,
    In its soft and silken wave,

Kindly nature's hushed to stillness,
  By the honored chieftain's grave,
Sweetly—silently he's sleeping,
  And upon the dewy air
Floats the sacred notes of angels,
  As his spirit hymns his prayer.
Silently the chieftain's sleeping—
  Bow the head and bend the knee—
Dare not disturb the silence,
  Here beneath this sacred tree

By EBEN E. REXFORD.

OH! Nation, weep thy bitterest tears
  Above the dear, departed dead.
Great deeds his memory endears,
  And round his name a glory shed.
Oh! Nation, weep! to thee he gave
  The boon of freedom, high and grand;
And now he fills a patriot's grave,
  A martyr for the sorrowing land.

Oh, Banner that he loved, no more
  His eyes on earth to thee will turn;
From where the heavenly standards soar,
  He'll look to see thy glories burn.
'Tis meet that thou shouldst weep to-day;
  So droop thy folds against the sky,
And mourn above the sacred clay,
  And put thy glad rejoicing by.

Oh! Bell, ring out thy saddest chimes,
　　Upon the mournful, listening air;
Each Northern heart with sorrow rhymes,
　　No bitterer pain the North could bear.
Ring out a sad and sweet refrain,
　　A requiem for the honored dead;
It will not raise to life again,
　　But wake sweet echoes o'er his head.

Oh! Eagle, in the empyreal air,
　　Bore thou his giant soul away,
To where the Lord's anointed are,
　　In God's unending glorious day?
His soul full oft, with Freedom's zeal,
　　Hath sped away on eagle's wings,
To where the hosts of Freedom kneel,
　　And where the souls of freemen sing.

His life hath been a beacon-light,
　　Through storm and gloomy night of war;
And now, when morn drives out the night,
　　He lives a higher life afar.
The end he strove to gain is won;
　　The hosts of treason overthrown;
At last, we trust, the night is done
　　With us—and him before the throne!

Oh, Freedman, mourn! he raised thee up
　　From years of toil and bondage sore,
He dashed aside the bitter cup,
　　And said that thou shouldst drink no more.

He gave to thee thy self and soul,
    And called thee by the name of MAN!
Upon your hearts his name enroll,
    As worker of the freedom plan.

The loss is not our loss alone!
    We lost a chieftain true and tried;
But freedom claims him for her own,
    With all a mother's tearful pride.
But many a heart across the sea,
    That breathed with him in freedom's air;
Will often say to memory,
    "We lost our noblest brother there."

Hail! chieftain, on the eternal shore.
    The whole world lost a friend in thee.
Still, freedom-haunted, hover o'er
    The sun-bright banner of the free.
Join hands with kindred souls on high,
    With those who fought in freedom's van;
And found it pleasure thus to die,
    In making free their fellow-man.

Oh! Nation, on thy tablets write
    The name of LINCOLN over all!
And wreathe in red, and blue, and white,
    The name beneath the funeral pall.
Fold o'er him, in his quiet rest,
    The grand old flag our fathers gave;
Yes, let it wrap his pulseless breast,
    Within the silence of the grave.

Oh! Nation, in the coming years,
   When Peace dwells with us all again,
Above his tomb we'll drop our tears,
   As summer clouds drop quiet rain.
We'll tell our children, by his grave,
   The deeds that made us love him so;
And of the blessed boon he gave;
   How blessed, every child shall know!

By LEAH, New Orleans.

HE is gone—gone for ever! go muffle the bell;
   Go weep, for few spirits like his shall depart;
Let the loud, mournful wail of a great nation tell—
   The grief that has shaken a nation's strong heart.
And bend the bright banner of freedom o'er him—
   So willing to guard it, so mighty to save;
Be its proud staff unshaken, its stars never dim—
   Save when drooping and moistened with tears at his grave.

In the midst of a tempest that threatened to tear
   The bonds of our mighty Republic in twain,
Like a guardian angel, his genius was there,
   Gath'ring the links to unite them again.
Ah! well may the heart of America mourn:
   An orb from her bright constellation has sped!
An oak from her forest of greatness is torn,
   A hue from her rainbow of glory has fled!

His spirit has left you, and gone to its home;
 Kneel, children of freedom, and weep o'er his dust;
Go call for another, but whence shall he come?
 There are many to answer, but few ye can trust.
For he stood midst the night of the storm-cloud unmoved,
 'Neath the lightning of hatred, unscathed by its shock,
While his heart ever clung to the Union he loved,
 As the roots of the pine-tree entwine round the rock.

The strong bark is shattered,—its wreck has swept on
 Where the billows of death in their mournfulness flow;
The rudder is lost, and the pilot has gone
 Where the winds of adversity never can blow.
He is gone! but his greatness has kindled a fire
 In the temple of fame, on Columbia's shore—
A beacon of glory that cannot expire
 'Till truth be forgotten and freedom's no more.

By GULA MEREDITH.

GO to that land where the martyrs await thee;
 Hark to their shouts as they welcome thee home:
There, in that clime, none shall harm thee or hate thee,
 For into heaven no *treason* dare come!

Go where the waters of life, ever flowing,
 Wash from the spirit all traces of sin;
Nevermore of the cares and the toils of earth knowing,
 Into thy rest, martyred one, enter in.

Into thy hands the "victor's palm" given;
  Placed on thy brow the circlet of gold;
Henceforth an heir of the glories of heaven,
  Thine shall be pleasures and rapture untold.

These are all thine! but for us that remaineth?
  We, who have known thee and loved thee for years?
Naught but the tomb that thy body containeth,
  And a sorrow that cannot be lightened by tears.

See! round thy tomb how a nation comes weeping;
  Hush ye your wailing and smother each moan;
Disturb not his rest where our martyr is sleeping;
  Enwrapped in his glory, go, leave him alone!

Soft o'er that tomb shall the winds whisper ever;
  Sweet shall the birds sing; the flowers bloom fair;
Enshrined in the hearts of thy people for ever,
  As sweet and as fresh shall thy memory be there!

———oo:o:oo———

By HENRY B. HIRST.

THE ground is white with apple blossoms,
  As though a fragrant snow lay there;
And from the meadows' breezy bosoms
  The blackbird's music floods the air;
But he, who heard the robin's whistle,
  Last spring, among the apple's bloom—
The liberator, priest, and saviour—
  The MARTYR! passes to his tomb.

Through the long avenues of cities,
  Through the commingling people's hum,
Marshalled by sighs, and sobs, and pities,
  The sacred relics onward come.
The very leaves themselves are weeping;
  While tears fill every earthly eye,
As mournfully the cortege, sweeping
  To solemn dirges, passes by.

Toll slowly, bells, toll very slowly,
  Murmur in moans a nation's woe;
Boom, minute guns, most melancholy,
  Heaven's thunder echoed from below.
Close every door, shut every casement,
  Drape every banner-fold with black,
Mourn, silent streets, from roof to basement,
  One passes hence to come not back.

Through the long cycles of the ages,
  Searching the catacombs of time,
Blazoned in gold on history's pages,
  No other name stands more sublime.
And since the awful crucifixion,
  And since the damned deed of Cain,
No record lives of such affliction,
  None greater numbered with the slain.

The ground is white with apple blossoms,
  As though a fragrant snow lay there;
And from the meadows' breezy bosoms
  The blackbird's music floods the air.

But he, who heard the robin's whistle,
  Last spring, among the apple's bloom,
The liberator, priest, and saviour—
  The MARTYR! passes to his tomb.

By S. B. H———.

HARK! from New England's vine-clad hills,
    The birth-place of the free,
And from our noble prairie land,
    The home of Liberty,
A wail of sorrow fills the air,
    For deed of murder done,
Staining the flag that proudly spreads
    Her eagle toward the sun.

Staining the noble heritage
    For which our fathers bled—
Staining with deeper dye the land
    Where sleeps the mighty dead,
Who won the regal crown she wore,
    And placed it on her brow—
Alas, for proud Columbia's name!
    'Tis soiled—'tis tarnished now.

The martyr sleeps—his stalwart arm
    Is meekly folded o'er
The heart that throbbed for human woes,
    But it shall throb no more.

The hand is still—the visage marred,
  In placid silence lies;
The silvery locks are parted o'er,
  And closed the sightless eyes.

The martyr sleeps—but he hath borne
  The cry of the oppressed
Up to the great Jehovah's throne,
  And passed into his rest.
He sleeps—but from his dust shall rise
  The birth-cry of the free,
And o'er his peaceful grave shall rest
  The star of Liberty.

By H. A. L———.

THY ways, O God, are strange to us,
  We cannot find them out;
Oh! give us faith to hope and trust,
  That we may never doubt.

Our hearts are sad—the nation mourns
  Its great and noble chief;
And over all the land there rolls
  The surges of its grief.

"With charity to all," he breathed
  His gentle life away,
And left a fragrance pure and sweet
  As flowers of balmy May.

"With charity to all,"—to thee,
   O! fiend, who dealt the blow
Which plunged the land in bitter tears,
   This charity did flow.

"With charity to all,"—to thee,
   Thou spirit of the pit,
To thee, which made us thus to mourn,
   And in sackcloth to sit.

O! justice, let thy sword be swift
   To punish such a deed!
O! earth in sorrow bow thy head,
   And for our country plead!

By R. M. JOHNSON.

HEAR! ten thousand bells reveal it!
   See! a million shrouded banners seal it!
Twice ten million hearts do feel it!—
               Lincoln is dead!

When the nation freedom's song is singing—
While the echo far and wide is ringing—
"Peace on earth," and mercy to them bringing—
               Lincoln is dead!

When the noblest victory of the ages,
Marks our nation's grand historic pages,
Honest leaders! purest of her band of sages—
               Lincoln is dead!

He, who in compassion often shielded;
Who a mighty vengeance could have wielded,
Ere the traitor demons hardly yielded—
                Lincoln is dead!

Never blood of man so precious given,
Never hearts so many sorely riven,
Save for Him who purchased heaven—
                Lincoln is dead!

God is teaching in this trying hour,
And we yet may see His mighty power
In the justice that shall quickly lower—
                Lincoln is dead!

By the martyred brave, who liberty defended;
By his hand, struck down when mercifully extended,
Let us swear that traitors' days shall now be ended—
                Lincoln is dead!

By WM. BOYLAN.

ILLUSTRIOUS martyr!—friend of the oppress'd,
Thy ashes we bear to the far distant West,
To lay 'neath the sod of your own native soil—
Patriot, statesman, and true son of toil.

Thy mem'ry we cherish—it shall ne'er be forgot;
Our deliverer!—the victim of treason's foul plot—
In thy look could be seen the last dying word,
"They know not what they do, forgive them, O Lord."

The prayer of the bondman went up night and day,
"Lord, send us a Moses to show us the way."
Like Moses of old, thou didst lead them safe through,
Till the fair land of Canaan each pilgrim could view.

While a nation rejoiced at the bright dawn of peace,
When bloodshed, and carnage, and murder should cease.
The assassin, with dagger and pistol in hand,
Spread a pall of deep mourning all over the land.
Did he think that by taking thy innocent life
He would thus put an end to this terrible strife?
No; it united all freemen as one solid rock
To grind all to powder who dare stand its shock.

Past ages their heroes and martyrs may boast,
The future may furnish a still greater host;
But when the historian the long roll shall call,
The name of A. LINCOLN shall tower above all.

By Rev. ALEX. CLARK.

THE Lord is near! with Sinai tread
    He comes to earth again;
From sudden darkness overhead,
A tongue of lightning, clear and dread,
Enough to wake the dusty dead,
    Proclaims God's will to men.

Oh, bleeding country! now arise,
    And call upon the Lord.

Thy broken heart and tearful eyes
Win pity on thee from the skies,
Through Christ, the world's slain sacrifice,
   Who saves thee by His word.

Thou God of nations; hear our prayer;
   We lift our thoughts to Thee;
Our sinful nation's life, oh, spare!
And may our grief Thy grace declare,
By every Christly cross we bear,
   To bless and make men free!

By UMBRA.

THE hour is past—the deed is done!
   A nation mourns a ruler gone!
         His life is sped.
The news has flashed along the wires,
And in each loyal heart inspires
         A sense of dread.

And shall the sword of justice sleep,
The while we stand and idly weep,
         With 'bated breath?
No! "By the Eternal," let us swear
That we are freemen still, and dare
         Avenge his death.

And, vainly though the murderer try,
By many a deep-laid scheme, to fly
         A nation's wrath;

The thousands who are brave and true,
With hearts to will, and hands to do,
    Beset his path.

For, through the tears we vainly weep,
A cry for *vengeance* comes, with deep
    Resistless power;
And though a cloud is on each brow,
That broods in sadness o'er it now,
    We bide the hour.

By M. G. HALPINE.

LET victory her shining forehead veil,
  And let the flag, he loved so well, droop low!
Seen through our tears, its starry field grows pale,
  Draped with the symbol of a nation's woe!
It was not his to fall with those who led
  The van, where, now, its folds wave broad and free,
And yet not one of all our martyred dead
  Has died a braver, nobler death than he!

Although, at noon, has set his glorious sun,
  Let not our hearts grow faint, our faith wax dim;
Nor weakly grieve, as tho' he left undone
  The weighty task the Master gave to him.
Like Him, whose cause he served, whose home he shares,
  It was his solemn work, his mission high,
Through weary months to bear a nation's cares,—
  Then, for the holy truths he taught, *to die!*

Our chosen Moses has passed on before;
  Yet, ere his footsteps touched the shining strand,
He saw the star of freedom rise once more,—
  From Pisgah's mount he viewed the promised land!
E'en at the best, frail children of the dust,
  Oft must we "walk by faith and not by sight;"
Still must we feel that He, in whom we trust,
  However dark the way, will lead us right.

If it shall join, as one, each sorrowing heart
  To finish *well* the work his hand begun;
If it a higher, purer zeal impart,
  His death may do more than his life has done!
For, by the tears we shed, the shame we feel,
  This fearful gloom, with grief and horror rife,
We learn no light and careless touch can heal
  The treacherous wound that sought a nation's life!

ANONYMOUS.

A NATION grieves—'tis sorrow's night,—
  Yet says "God's will be done!"
Arraigning not th' Eternal's might,
  She mourns her martyr son,
In triumph's hour, with loud acclaim,
  Her banners sought the sky,
But midst her joy affliction came—
  Her flag is half-mast high.

Too well th' assassin's hand prevailed
  O'er him, the staunch and true,
Whom faction's arms in vain assailed—
  He braved the tempest through.
Not only in his country's bound,
  Goes forth the bitter cry;
For him in sorrowing nations round,
  The flag is half-mast high.

When discord hurled her ruthless brand
  Where peace all smiling reigned,
And war with fratricidal hand
  Columbia's soil profaned,
Aloft he held with giant limb
  Her flag while storms passed by,
And only now, in grief for him,
  That flag is half-mast high.

He loved and sought his country's fame—
  Proud might to her he gave—
He lived and earned a patriot's name—
  He found a martyr's grave.
Columbia's son! while by his tomb
  Thou stand'st with tear-dimmed eye,
Resolve to live like him for whom
  The flag's now half-mast high.

Montreal, Canada.

THE BLOSSOM OF THE SOUTH.

By INA D. COOLBRITH.

WHILE yet the land was young,
    The planter of the South flung forth a seed:
      "A goodly tree!" he said,
Although, indeed, we called it but a weed;
Till by the hot soil warmed and nourished,
    Up to the light it sprung.

    'Twas cause for wondering,
How that land yet moistened with the blood
    Of freedom's brotherhood—
That plucked, in God's own name, the starry gem
Of liberty from England's diadem—
    Could bear so foul a thing.

    Yet year by year it grew,
And put forth leaves. And they did nurture it
With the tears and blood of bondage, and the sweat
Wrung from the forehead of the slave,
    And still no heed we gave;
Until its branches spread on either hand,
    And over half the land
      Their baleful shadow threw.

    And so it stood, at last,
An evil thing that could no longer hide
From the strong north wind; for its poisonous dew

Rained on our temples, and from every leaf
There hissed a serpent-challenge! Would ye know
How answered? It is written far and wide,
By the fierce hand of war, on field and plain
   Heaped with the nation's slain!
Answered in deeds whose memory shall last
   Till time itself be past!

But oh, not yet the tree has ripened,
And the full bud expanded to the flower!
   Lo! in our trial hour
God gave to us a leader: pure and true
His great heart was, as the great cause he led—
And led to victory! And the people knew
His worth, and loved him: placing its strong hand
In his, as fearless as a little child
Within its sire's. Stainless and undefiled
He stood erect—God's chosen to command!

   The Southron sowed the seed,
That to-day opened in a flower blood-red!
Within whose deadly leaves there lurked a deed
   To shake a world with grief.
A Southron plucked the blooms, and garlanded,
And placed them on the forehead of our chief!

   Oh, reapers of the North!
Ye know it now—the tree with all its fruit,
   Have ye not sickles keen and strong? Go forth!
The branches droop, indeed, but the foul root
   Still festers in the soil; and God has said

The land is His, and must be purified!
So when once more Columbia lifts her head,
Worthy to be called free, and wears in pride
Her lily-crown of peace, shall we not bring,
First, to Jehovah's throne an offering—
Next, to the tomb where rests the honored head
Of our beloved dead?

San Francisco.

By KATIE W. NICHOLS.

THROUGH four sad sacrificial years,
Rivers have poured of blood and tears;
And now with sudden grief oppressed,
We yield our dearest and our best.

One traitor hand—one direful blow—
Has plunged unnumbered hearts in woe:
From Eastern shore to Western steeps,
Lo! the whole stricken nation weeps.

OUR LEADER—when thy blood was shed,
When thou didst join the honored dead,
On Freedom's altar we laid down
Of all our sacrifice—the crown.

Alas! that his most precious blood
Should mingle with the crimson flood,
In whose remedial mighty tide
A nation's guilt is purified.

He led us till the weary night
Was yielding to the longed-for light;
He caught the dawn's first kindling ray,
Then entered heaven's eternal day!

Our Moses he—whose faithful hand
Led us so near the promised land:
He saw its distant palm trees wave—
We strew their branches o'er his grave!

Oh, dearly loved and martyred one!
Our country's second WASHINGTON!
Thy children come in silent gloom,
And weep to-day around thy tomb!

Our hearts are buried there with thee:
Forever fresh thy memory be;
For loving hearts till time shall end
Shall bless thy name as FREEDOM'S FRIEND!

From that fresh grave we turn away
With saddened hearts, to kneel and pray
That in the future we may see
God chooses wiser far than we.

By L. W. F——.

BUT yester night the joyous bells
    Pealed out their gladsome strain,
And cannons thundered forth their glee,
Till echo sent the jubilee
    O'er valley, hill and plain.

And starry banners waved aloft,
   And patriot shout and boast
Were heard exultant through the land,
For glorious victories, great and grand,
   Had crowned our gallant host.

But now, alas! the nation's joy
   Is turned to direst grief;
The exultant shout—a wail of woe,
Instead of mirth—our tears now flow
   For him, the nation's chief.

Cut down in all his glorious strength,
   Our country's earthly guide,
A Joshua o'er our valiant band,
To lead us to that promised land
   Of peace; where we'd abide.

But God, who rules and reigns o'er all,
   Hath dealt the blow in love.
The work He gave him to do,
He faithfully has carried through,
   And wears the crown above.

Altho' a cruel murderous foe
   His precious life-blood drains,
Though traitors seek our country's doom,
And everything seems wrapt in gloom,
   We still believe *God reigns.*

THE PRESIDENT'S DREAM.

By BENJAMIN FRANKLIN TAYLOR.

ATHWART the troubled waters swiftly sailing
    Thou saw'st the phantom vessel cleave its way:
Around its path the wandering winds were wailing,
    And white around it flashed the angry spray.
Alas! it flitted o'er a troubled ocean
    Where withering winds swept wildly as it past,
And urged it onward with unquiet motion,
    Tossed by the tempest long—but moored at last.

'Twas but the emblem of the swiftly gliding
    And waning hours of thy imperilled life,
The briefness of thy glorious day betiding,
    Thou pilot on the sea of freedom's strife!
Thou too wert battling with the tempest's power:
    Thine too a pathway o'er a stormy deep;
But now the port is gained, no storm-clouds lower,
    The bark is safe—oh! faithful pilot, sleep!

As the swift ships that on the far-off waters
    Wax dim and vanish—so we pass away
From life's sad ocean—so earth's sons and daughters
    Fade like the shadows of the dying day;
But thou, our chief! hast left a noble story
    Of truth and triumph for our sons to tell,
Thy vanished bark hath left a wake of glory
    To follow thee along time's ocean swell.

Thou wert the vessel first God's message bringing,
　　Glad news of freedom to Columbia's strand,
From Afric's sons the tyrant's fetters wringing,
　　"Proclaiming liberty throughout the land."
Oh, now no blot of slavery shall stain us!
　　Henceforth we stand, a commonwealth *all* free!
Thou wert the first that blessed boon to gain us,
　　Oh, martyr on the shrine of liberty!

Thy bark hath faded from earth's gloomy water;
　　Safe moored where never clouds nor storms arise,
Far from these billowy wastes all red with slaughter,
　　Thy post is won—the haven of the skies.
Thy sail is furled amid celestial islands,
　　'Neath fadeless sunlight and eternal day;
Why should we mourn that to those glorious skylands,
　　From troubled shores, the swift ship fled away?

Not unto thee—to us—belongs the sighing,
　　The wail of anguish and the falling tear!
Not unto thee—to us—the pang—the dying
　　Of proud hopes sinking withered by thy bier.
Ours the wild dirge—the shrouded flag—the weeping—
　　The death-bell tolling from the sombre dome;
Thine, the loved form in stilly grandeur sleeping,
　　The crown of glory, and the heavenly home.

ANONYMOUS.

As orphans round the mournful bier
 Where rests a father's head,
Stand silent, while the glistening tear
 Falls hot above the dead;
So we, a nation orphaned now,
 Our hearts with anguish rent,
Stand, one great weeping family,
 By our dead President.

He was our MOSES; through the sea
 Red with fraternal blood,
He led our nation, while our foe
 Sank in the angry flood.
Through this dark wilderness of war,
 Light from his face has shone,
As from some Sinai's burning top,
 He came a prophet down.

His voice in clarion notes rang out
 The bondman's jubilee;
His name is on the freedman's tongue,
 Watchword of liberty.
Thy might, O God, was in his heart;
 Thy wisdom made him wise;
He lived a man—he ruled a prince—
 He died a sacrifice.

O Lord, is this Thy hand divine
 That holds the bitter rod?

Help us to bow and kiss Thy hand,
  Our chastening, loving God.
Anoint for us with oil of grace
  Our JOSHUA—who shall stand,
Our Israel safe, this Jordan crossed,
  In the glad promised land.

ANONYMOUS.

TOLL! Toll! Toll!
 On every hand,
Ye bells, throughout the land;
Our noble leader in his glory lies,
The damp of death upon his sealed eyes—
A martyr true to liberty he dies.
 Toll! Toll! Toll!

 Weep! Weep! Weep!
On every hand,
Ye heroes of the land;
Our chieftain's dead.
Great God! and must it be?
Alas, how brief is our mortality!
Our Father, help and bless to us this agony.
 Weep! Weep! Weep!

 Mourn! Mourn! Mourn!
On every hand,
Ye patriots of the land;

No more his honest face will greet the sun—
His day is finished and his work is done:
A crown of glory rests his brow upon.
    Mourn! Mourn! Mourn!

By EDWARD P. NOWELL.

OH, what a ghastly, bleeding wound
    The nation suffers from this day!
Throughout the land is heard no sound,
    Save sorrow's dirge of deep dismay!

Most honored chief! We mourn his loss
    Far more than anguished heart can tell;
We bow beneath the cumbrous cross
    Upborne for him we loved so well!

His wisdom, truth, fidelity,
    Rejoiced us with his just renown;
Woe, woe! that man so base should be,
    As dastardly to strike him down!

True freedom's martyr! tears of grief
    In floods from sorrow's clouds outpour,
Bedewing joy's rich harvest sheaf,
    Ere safe within fruition's store.

Will bitter tears e'er be repressed?
    Can joy relume our hearts again?
Shall sighs control the harrowed breast?
    Must pleasure be usurped by pain?

Almighty Father! Thou our trust!
We ever in Thy grace repose;
Dear Saviour! raise us from the dust,
Assuage our grief and heal our woes!

By C. R. B——.

GOD of our fathers, hear,
　To Thee we lift our prayer
　　In danger's hour;
Now while the tempests rave
Over the land and wave,
Do Thou the nation save;
　　Thou hast the power.

Where the fierce battle-stroke
Rolls up its sulphur smoke,
　　Blotting the sky;
'Mid the wild conflict's roar,
Where war's red torrents pour,
Clotting the fields with gore;
　　God, hear the cry.

Stay Thou the tears and blood
That roll a purple flood
　　O'er all the land.
Oh, mark the widow's sigh,
Oh, hear the orphan's cry,
And, from Thy throne on high,
　　Deliv'rance send.

Oh, bid our warrings cease,
Let the sweet dove of peace
   On us descend.
Hear the oppressed complain,
Break every tyrant's chain,
Rend every bond in twain,
   Bid thraldom end.

By THOMAS WARD.

HE died with mercy on his lips
   As the dread need to ask it came:
When could he go with better grace
   That mercy of his God to claim?

He fell surrendering to his Lord
   The vengeance-bolt within his hand:
What pardon-plea could sinner make
   Like such submission to command?

Strong was his will to serve the State,
   And strong his arm to break the foe,
Most strong his manly tenderness
   When the opposer was laid low.

Then rest, great heart, in humble hope!
   The follower in his Master's way
Finds advocates in good men's tongues
   And friendly Judge on trial-day.

By SAM. WHITING.

WELL may the nation mourn for him,
    Who lies in death's embraces low,
Whose kindly-beaming glance is dim,
    Whose fate has filled all hearts with woe.

We follow him from humble youth,
    Up to his manhood's riper years;
How radiant, in the light of truth,
    The history of his life appears!

Called by his country to the helm,
    As pilot of our Ship of State,
When storms seemed destined to o'erwhelm,
    And our proud foes were all elate:

How grandly we beheld him rise
    Above all bitter party strife!
He saw but one alluring prize—
    His darling country's rescued life.

Through all this strife of civil war,
    With faction's blood-hounds on his track,
He sought to heal the nation's sore,
    To win the rebel leaders back.

Oh! traitors to your native land,
    Behold the lessons you have taught
In the assassin's blood-stained hand—
    In this deep woe your deeds have wrought.

A nobler heart than his ne'er beat—
    He broke the fetters off the slave—
His soul may, at the mercy-seat,
    With full assurance mercy crave.

The tender heart is cold in death,
    The loving eyes are closed for aye,
The nation stands with bated breath,
    While peals the wild funereal cry.

Bear the dead martyr to his rest,
    Far from the scene of bloody crime;
Earth's noblest will his worth attest,
    And consecrate through future time.

"Mercy to those who mercy show,"
    Now let the murd'rous rebels feel
How heavy falls the avenging blow
    From justice with her hand of steel.

By Miss S. A. M'CAFFREY.

GOD save Columbia,
    Still free and glorious;
Save our loved land;
    Let strife and carnage cease,
    From direful war release,
    O God, now grant us peace!
Save, save our land.

God save Columbia!
    Our fathers bled and died

    For thy dear land;
        Thou who didst make us free
        From Britain's tyranny,
        All hearts now cry to Thee,
God save our land!

God save Columbia,
        Her altars and firesides;
God save our land;
        Let love, not hate, prevail,
        Be hushed the mourner's wail;
        Thy strong arm cannot fail;
Save, save our land.

God save Columbia,
        Shield her lov'd stripes and stars;
God save our land;
        Stretch thine arm over us,
        Make us victorious!
        Still free and glorious;
God save our land.

By ADOLPH ANCKER.

AY! burst with grief your cannon's iron throats,
    And hurl their thunders on the morning air;
Upon your bells toll only saddest notes,
    For him ye mourn who never more shall hear.

Shroud all your banners in the deepest woe,
    With fun'ral dirges make the air resound;

Let labor, too, its 'custom'd toil forego,
    And *feel* the melancholy hov'ring 'round.

Soon will the grave the patriot martyr claim,
    His soul an off'ring to almighty truth;
Nations unborn shall emulate his fame,
    Forever glowing, with immortal youth.

Pray God that from his ashes may arise
    Another soul as noble, pure and great;
Another Lincoln, whose far-searching eyes
    May find the safe path for the Ship of State.

High o'er his bones the sculptur'd marble raise;
    And oh! ye vot'ries of the tuneful nine,
Give to the great one his *just* meed of praise
    In better verse than these poor lines of mine.

By EMMA BENTON BENNETT.

ONWARD and upward, martial strains,
    Float o'er our dear transcendent plains,
Compressing music into woe,
Sighing more soft as far ye go,
Scarce soothing hearts that sorely mourn—
A nation by his power upborne,
Who broke the fetters of the slave,
To consecrate our LINCOLN'S grave!

Discourse the airs he loved the best,
Before we lay him there to rest,

Where all the sweets of prairie flowers,
And melodies from birdling bowers,
Shall year by year, in song and bloom,
Surround his calm immortal tomb;
Where they of every age and clime
Shall come to think and grow sublime!

Dead marches seem unfitting now,
When such a patriot's form is low;
The country he has served so well
Prolongs a deep funereal knell,
But through its mighty agony
Millions remember they are free!
And sing, "Columbia, happy land,"
A chastened but a stronger band.

ANONYMOUS.

THE joyous bells rang through the land,
    And every heart was beating high,
Friends clasped each other by the hand,
    And tears of joy dimmed many an eye;
For after four long years of war,
    Rebellion tottered to its base—
Richmond is ours! Our toils are o'er!
    Soon peace will show her smiling face!

And he who through the direful strife,
    So wise, so well had borne his part,
Had saved from harm the nation's life,
    Was taken to the nation's heart;

The cannon roared, the bells were swung,
   And praise from all to him was given,
His name was heard on every tongue,
   And blessings bore it up to heaven.

Alas! each heart is filled with woe—
   Our joy is changed to saddest grief,
A dastard's hand, a secret foe,
   Has slain the man who was our chief;
The minute guns boom through each town,
   The joyous bells now sadly toll,
The blow which struck our ruler down
   Has reached, has pierced the nation's soul.

O Thou who canst alone restrain
   The wrath of man, we look to Thee,
Forgive us if we feel the pain
   Too great to bear; we cannot see
The end Thou seest; we blindly grope;
   Lead us, O God! lead us aright!
In Thee alone we trust, we hope;
   Unveil our eyes and show us light.

But he who now in death lies cold,
   The victim of rebellious hate,
Shall have his name full high enrolled
   With those whom men have called "the Great;"
'Twas for his country's cause he died,
   And thus with martyrs, heroes, sages,
His country will hand down with pride,
   His name through all the coming ages.

By F. P. GRIFFIN.

GREAT God! what shadows on our footsteps fall,
    Unutterable woes our spirits bend;
How beauteous hope and sharp appalling grief
    In quick strange contrast and succession blend.

The rosy hues of yester-morning's dawn
    Were full of promise, pregnant with delight;
Demoniac spirits now flit o'er the scene,
    Flame o'er the hideous landscape and obscure our sight.

Good heart, great friend of all the human race,
    Farewell—life's evanescent dream for thee is o'er;
A nation's overtasking toils and cumbrous cares
    Shall press thy brow and vex thy heart no more.

We need no marble bust or sculptured clay,
    Thy treasured glory, thy benignant fame to keep;
Resplendent honors cluster round thy name,
    And thy untimely end a nation's tears shall weep.

Farewell, pure spirit, freedom's champion thou,
    Endearing memories, and emotions cling
Around thy fate, while ages yet untold
    Their offerings to thy hallowed shrine will bring.

Time shall grow old and nations fade away,
    And many names upon fame's scroll now traced,
Forgot shall be, as if they ne'er had been,
    But thy illustrious record cannot be erased.

Thy name shall live of martyr'd heroes chief,
  Columbia's children garner by thy honored dust,
While angel watchers—heaven's embattled hosts,
  Shall guard with jealous care the sacred trust.

By Mrs. L. M. WILLIAMS.

FATHER of light and love!
  Thou, God! who reign'st above,
    Parent supreme!
To Thee our wishes tend,
Lowly our spirits bend,
Our Father, and our Friend,
    Guide Thou our theme.

Protect us by Thy power,
In this our dark'ning hour:
    Still, Thou, our fears.
Our nation's chief laid low—
Our hearts, with grief, o'erflow,
And swell with deep'ning woe,
    A nation's tears.

At freedom's shrine we bow;
Bending in suppliance now,
    Thy blessing crave.
Accept, great God! our King!
The sacrifice we bring;
One true heart offering,
    Our country save!

God! bless our native land,
Guide its victorious band
  In paths of peace.
Let no discordant sound
Within our hearts be found,
But truth and love abound,
  Till time shall cease.

ANONYMOUS.

HUSHED to-day are sounds of gladness
  From the mountain to the sea,
And the plaintive voice of sadness
  Rises, mighty God, to Thee.

Freedom claimed another martyr;
  Heaven receives another saint;
Who are we, Thy will to question?
  Lord, we weep without complaint.

May we, to Thy wisdom bowing,
  Own Thy love in this dark spell,
While, with tears, a mighty nation,
  Buries one they loved so well.

And O Thou! who took our leader,
  With the promised land in view,—
While on Pisgah's height we leave him,
  Lead us, Lord, the Jordan through.

By NATHAN UPHAM.

TOLL! toll the solemn bell!
    A great, good man is dead!
The nation loves him well,
    And bitter tears are shed;
O'er all the land, from wave to wave,
Will millions mourn the untimely grave!

Toll! toll the solemn bell!
    Enshroud the flag in gloom!
Can words the anguish tell,
    Or sunshine gild the tomb?
O'er all the land, from sea to sea,
Weep! lovers of fair liberty!

Toll! toll the solemn bell!
    We gaze on his dead face;
We feel his funeral knell
    A burning, deep disgrace.
O'er all the land, from gulf to lake,
Will slumbering justice now awake!

Toll! toll the solemn bell!
    We lay him sadly down!
God knew his virtues well,
    And set the martyr-crown!
O'er all the land we weep to-day—
Yet angels bore that soul away!

ANONYMOUS.

O THOU! who through the desert wilds
    Thy chosen people once did lead—
Who brought them safe to Horeb's rock,
    And manna gave in hour of need.

Be with us now, and hear the cry
    That rises from our stricken land;
Oh! lay Thy rod of judgment by—
    In mercy stay Thy chastening hand!

The pilot from our "Ship of State"
    In evil hour away is torn—
Oh! who shall guide her on her course
    As through the foaming waves she's borne?

The staff on which we fondly leaned,
    O Father! now, alas, is broke:
We own Thy goodness, power and love,
    But yet we weep the afflictive stroke.

The nation mourns the nation's loss—
    Our hearts are bowed in deepest grief;
With tear-dimmed eyes we turn to Thee—
    For Thou alone canst bring relief!

We humbly bow before Thy throne—
    Thy aid and blessing we implore—
Our bleeding country heal and save,
    And peace and union yet restore.

And grant, that though, like one of old,
  Our chief has laid his "mantle" by—
Upon some other it may fall,
  And fit him for his mission high!

ANONYMOUS.

TOLL, ye bells, a solemn dirge,
  Earth shall join the sad refrain;
And the sea's remotest surge,
  Moan for freedom's champion slain.

Veil thy radiance, glowing sun;
  Moon and stars, go out in gloom;
Weep, ye skies, for hopes undone,—
  Weep a kingly patriot's doom.

Banner worshipped by the brave—
  Fairest ensign of the free,
With thy sable emblems wave,
  Drooping low and mournfully.

Oh, ye vales and verdant isles!
  How can beauty gild ye so?
Why should ye be dres'd in smiles,
  When our human hearts o'erflow?

Is it some celestial beam
  From the gates of Paradise?
Is it Heaven's refulgent gleam,
  Half revealed to mortal eyes?

Wide unfold your scenes of light,
  Glorious realm, no pen can paint.
Welcome him, ye throngs in white,
  Crown him *hero*, MARTYR, SAINT.

By D. AMBROSE DAVIS.

OH, build a monument to him,
  And let it tower to heaven;
Praise God that for His noble child
  The manifest is given.

Ay, build the structure for all time,
  Nor give it any bound;
Let not its summit be the sky,
  Or basis be the ground;

But rear it to the sacred realms,
  Where angel spirits roam,
And let the sparkling gems of worth
  Illuminate its dome.

Then hang from heaven's apex down
  An everlasting scroll,
And let the glowing emblem be
  The light of a martyr soul!

TO THE NATION.

By E. T. S.

THY chief is dead! Ay, bow thy head
  And weep thy bitter tears;
He's loved thee so, through weal and woe,
  And calmed thy wildest fears.

A nation weeps. A hero sleeps
  Unmindful of their grief.
O God! be just; above the dust
  Of our noble patriot chief.

Oh, help us feel that Thou canst heal
  The direst, sorest wounds;
Be Thou our stay, and help us pray,
  "Thy will, not mine, be done."

By CORA LISLE.

O GOD! can it indeed be true,
  Is traitor's work so low,
That even our pure and honest chief
  Must fall beneath its blow?

MURDERED! Alas, too true,
  Iscariot's spirit still
Doth rule the hearts of men,
  To do Satan's own will.

A murdered President,
  The land listens with dread.
To the awful tale of death,
  From town to village spread.

Our PRESIDENT, throughout the length
  Of the past four years of war,
How, ever onward, for the best,
  The nation's cause he bore.

Slain in the midst of those
  Who loved to speak his name,
Who faithful guardians were,
  Of his unspotted fame.

The cup of bitterness seems full,
  Tears spring from many an eye
That, save for such a grief as this,
  Would ever have been dry.

The name of LINCOLN is engraved
  In millions of loyal hearts,
Bright with the noble memory
  Which his record imparts.

By R. B. W.

OUR country's favorite, killed by murderous hand,
  In deepest grief has plunged our loyal land,
Gone from all cares of state to his last rest,
Since WASHINGTON, the purest and the best;

But he shall sink not in oblivion's waves
Who struck the shackles from a race of slaves!

A thousand virtues his, and but one fault,
And that by many deem'd what does exalt
The mind—the having too much mercy blent
With justice,—for he was *too lenient;*
His the large heart, too ready to forgive—
O, noble LINCOLN! hast thou ceased to live?—
Alas! the doleful tidings are too true,
Th' assassin's hand thy life-blood did imbrue!

And did God give us him to work His plan,
To free a race, give equal rights to man,
To guide a country through a sea of blood,
Conciliate the weak, assure the good:
This done, and light just breaking into day,
Was it God's will to call him thus away?—
Inscrutable and wise his every plan and way!

Oh ye, who, ere this, have contemned the one
Who now lays low with all his trials done,
And who have sympathized with Slavery's power
And traitors, in our country's darkest hour,—
Can ye not see that barbarism and wrong,
That murder, treason, ignorance, belong
To that curst institution you uphold,
And whose dark record, who can all unfold?
Oh! can you witness this its latest stain
And still for it your sympathies retain?
If so, oh! never hope heaven's blissful realm to gain!

O, ABRAHAM LINCOLN! martyr to the cause
Of justice, liberty, and righteous laws!
Adored, revered, by nations,—by the earth,
His name shall live, his wisdom and his worth,
And unborn hosts shall bless the day that gave him birth!

And when shall cease to give its light the sun,
When life and earth and time their race have run,
Then LINCOLN'S fame will cease,—with that of WASH-
INGTON!

By ENOLA.

THE badge, the drapery of woe
    Floats out upon the air;
And it is no unmeaning show,
    For grief is everywhere.

When, like the wind, from shore to shore,
    The fearful tidings ran,
It pierced the nation to its core,
    And wrung a cry of pain.

Each household felt as if a friend
    Had from its midst been torn;
They see "one vacant chair," and bend
    To weep, and sigh, and mourn.

There's scarce a house in all the land
    But wears the badge of woe,
There's not a heart however hard
    But feels the dreadful blow.

Oh, never did the world before
   Behold such wide-spread grief,
Hard hearts by sin all crusted o'er,
   Have wept to find relief.

And softer, purer hearts will keep
   "The memory of the just,"
And he shall live, who is asleep
   Low in the silent dust.

No, never can they make him die,
   The brave, good man we mourn,
Forever in the nation's heart
   His image will be borne.

Wherever truth and justice reign,
   And right prevails o'er wrong,
And honesty is loved, his name
   Will live the great among.

We would have had him live to reap
   A harvest in the land;
We hoped, when peace should smile again,
   To grasp his honest hand.

But He who rules in all the earth,
   Has interposed His will—
Oh! may He calm our smitten hearts,
   And whisper, "Peace, be still."

From the LONDON "FUN."

THE hand of an assassin, glowing red,
    Shot like a firebrand through the western sky;
And stalwart Abraham Lincoln now is dead!
    Oh! felon heart that thus could basely dye
The name of southerner with murderous gore!
    Could such a spirit come from mortal womb?
And what possessed it that not heretofore
    It linked its coward mission with the tomb?
Lincoln! thy fame shall sound through many an age,
    To prove that genius lives in humble birth;
Thy name shall sound upon historic page,
    For 'midst thy faults we all esteemed thy worth.
Gone art thou now! no more 'midst angry heat
    Shall thy calm spirit rule the surging tide,
Which rolls where two contending nations meet,
    To still the passion and to curb the pride.
Nations have looked and seen the fate of kings,
    Protectors, emperors, and such like men;
Behold the man whose dirge all Europe sings,
    Now past the eulogy of mortal pen!
He, like a lighthouse, fell athwart the strand;
Let curses rest upon the assassin's hand!

ANONYMOUS.

THERE'S a burden of grief on the breezes of spring,
    And a song of regret from the bird on its wing;
There's a pall on the sunshine and over the flowers,
And a shadow of graves on these spirits of ours;

For a star hath gone out from the night of our sky,
On whose brightness we gazed as the war-cloud roll'd
　　by;
So tranquil, and steady, and clear were its beams,
That they fell like a vision of peace on our dreams.

A heart that we knew had been true to our weal,
And a hand that was steadily guiding the wheel;
A name never tarnished by falsehood or wrong,
That had dwelt in our hearts like a soul-stirring song;
Ah! that pure, noble spirit has gone to its rest,
And the true hand lies nerveless and cold on his breast;
But the name and the memory—*these* never will die,
But grow brighter and dearer as ages go by.

Yet the tears of a nation fall over the dead,
Such tears as a nation before never shed;
For our cherished one fell by a dastardly hand,
A martyr to truth and the cause of the land;
And a sorrow has surged, like the waves to the shore,
When the breath of the tempest is sweeping them o'er,
And the heads of the lofty and lowly have bowed,
As the shaft of the lightning sped out from the cloud.

Not gathered, like Washington, home to his rest,
When the sun of his life was far down in the West;
But stricken from earth in the midst of his years,
With the Canaan in view, of his prayers and his tears.
And the people, whose hearts in the wilderness failed,
Sometimes, when the star of their promise had paled,

Now, stand by his side on the mount of his fame,
And yield him their hearts in a grateful acclaim.

Yet there on the mountain our leader must die,
With the fair land of promise spread out to his eye;
His work is accomplished, and what he has done
Will stand as a monument under the sun;
And his name, reaching down through the ages of time,
Will still through the years of eternity shine—
Like a star, sailing on through the depths of the blue,
On whose brightness we gaze every evening anew.

His white tent is pitched on the beautiful plain,
Where the tumult of battle comes never again;
Where the smoke of the war-cloud ne'er darkens the air,
Nor falls on the spirit a shadow of care.
The songs of the ransomed enrapture his ear,
And he heeds not the dirges that roll for him here;
In the calm of his spirit, so strange and sublime,
He is lifted far over the discords of time.

Then bear home gently, great son of the West—
'Mid her fair blooming prairies lay Lincoln to rest;
From the nation who loved him, she takes to her trust,
And will tenderly garner the consecrate dust.
A Mecca his grave to the people shall be,
And a shrine evermore for the hearts of the free.

MEMORY OF ABRAHAM LINCOLN.

By S. C. MERCER.

SOFT breathe the vernal winds, the sky is fair,
And April's fragrance scents the dewy air.
Yon heaven looks down on earth with eyes as mild
As a young mother's on her sleeping child,
Jealous lest aught should break her infant's calm,
And lulling its soft slumbers with a psalm.
So soft, so holy, comes the forest hymn,
From yon fair hill-tops, misty, blue and dim,
While war's discordant tumult seems to cease
In the sweet music of returning peace.

Yet where the fount of joy in crystal springs,
Some venomed asp its rankling poison flings;
And where the violets shed their fragrant breath
The night-shade pours the blistering dews of death.

What bloody phantom with a brow of wrath
Stalks in the van of our triumphal path,
And o'er our banners flings a funeral veil,
Till heaven grows black and mortal cheeks grow pale?
'Twas in the halls of mirth, a gala night,
Bright lamps o'er joyous thousands shed their light,
The nation's father sat amid the throng,
Relaxed his brow and heard the festal song;
He dreams not of conspiracy, nor sees
Above his head the sword of Damocles;
Wide opes the sepulchre its marble jaws,
All nature seems to make a breathless pause;

The deadly aim is made—the death-shot flies,
And freedom's martyr passes to the skies.

O, statesman, hero, patriot, friend, and sire,
Now the pale tenant of a funeral pyre,
Whose red right hand four years has held the rod,
The minister of freedom and of God,
Yet with the rod the blooming olive held,
While the dark deluge of rebellion swelled
And thundered round our ark—an argosy
More precious than the jewels of the sea,
And still with outstretched arms essayed to save
The ship-wrecked seamen from the yawning wave—
Thy love was strong as woman's—who, like thee,
Their interceding angel now shall be?

A genial wit, a homely native sense,
Nearer to truth than studied eloquence;
A quiet courage to defend the right,
And leave to heaven the issue of the fight;
A will of adamant, which seemed to be
The very flower of maiden modesty;
A conscience, holding truth of greater worth
Than all the crowns and treasures of the earth;
A love, whose strong affections seemed to bind,
In one the happiness of all mankind;
These were the jewels whose celestial flame
Shall burn with quenchless glow round LINCOLN's name;
The virtues which shall make his memory dear,
While justice reigns in yon eternal sphere.

And millions shall lament, with honest grief,
The people's friend, and freedom's fallen chief;
The huntsman shall forget the eager chase,
And pause to wipe his weather-beaten face;
The daring sailor on the distant sea,
Shall shed a tear-drop to his memory;
The widow's tears shall quench her cottage fire,
The soldier's orphan mourn his second sire.
There needs no glittering trappings of the tomb,
Nor martial dirge, nor hearse with nodding plume,
To tell their grief; but words devoid of art,
Show how this stroke has pierced the nation's heart.
Precious the tears shall be, the nation weeps,
And sacred be the sod where LINCOLN sleeps.
His fame shall be the jewel of the West,
Like a rich pearl on beauty's throbbing breast.
Mourn, O, ye mountains!—altars of the sky—
Fit monuments of him who cannot die;
Mourn, loud Atlantic! let thy thunder-dirge
Chant the sad requiem with Pacific's surge.
Mourn, O, New England! on thy granite base;
Mourn, Illinois, thy desolate dwelling-place;
Kentucky mourn! thy second God-like son
Sleeps in the dust, life's duty nobly done;
Mourn, Tennessee! the hero of the age
Sleeps with the Lion of the Hermitage;
Chanted the melancholy song shall be,
By all thy streams which hasten to the sea,
While Nashville's echoing wall of cedared hills,
With mournful cadence all the valley fills.

By C. H. WEBB.

THE pines are green on Shasta,
  No palm-tree's leaf is sere;
But a noble oak has fallen
  In this springtime of the year.
You may journey to the sunset,
  And from sunset to the sea,
But you'll find not in the forest,
  So stout, so brave a tree.

It stood the wrath of winter,
  The blinding sleet and snow;
And now the axe of treason
  Has laid the good tree low.
It was hard that in the springtime,
  When the blue was in the sky,
And the winter's worst was weathered,
  This good, stout tree should die.

But, though the hands of traitors
  Have hewn their murderous will;
Though the monarch tree lies prostrate,
  It all is live oak still!
And will furnish a firm keelson
  For our noble Ship of State,
And a scaffold where foul traitors
  Shall meet with traitors' fate.

Rest, Lincoln, in thy glory;
  Though slain by stealth you die,

Up, yonder, 'mong the stars,
　They ask not how, but why.
A more than warrior's wreath,
　A more than martyr's crown,
Thy foes pressed on thy brow—
　Rest in thy great renown!

San Francisco.

ANONYMOUS.

THE bells rang out
　A hoarse alarum from each brazen throat,
A hasty summons in each jangling note,
Four years ago this sacred Easter-tide,
Filling the land with consternation wide,
Telling of outraged law and war begun,
And all the loyal myriads as one
Gave back a shout!

Again they rang,
Once 'neath a chilly, gray, autumnal sky,
Once when midsummer's sun was throned on high,
Calling old men and boys to meet the foe,
And torn with doubts and fears, we saw them go,—
The battle raging at our very door,
Our peaceful hills scared by the cannon's roar
With iron clang.

One week ago
They rang with joyful peal at dead of night,
And every window blazed with sudden light,

Victorious salvoes thundered in our ears,
Triumphant shouts were choked by thankful tears,
While in the silent spaces far above,
Were heard the pinions of th' Eternal Dove
Descending slow.

To-day they toll:
Amazed with grief and horror is the land—
Dead!—dead!—and slain by an assassin's hand!
Dead—slain—the wisest, humblest, bravest, best,
Most christian chief a people e'er possessed!
Twice consecrated, twice the nation's choice,
In sorrow and in prayer it lifts its voice—
God keep his soul!

O martyred head!
So long with heaviest care and thought oppressed,
O heart divine within a human breast,
Ye are at peace! God granted you to know
Your labor crowned and perfect here below,
And now your toil is o'er, and humbly we
Own all the mercy of His strange decree
And mandate dread.

But ye—accursed!
Ye who have robbed us of our hope and guide,
Look to yourselves! In all the whole world wide
Lives not another who can step between
You and your retribution, or can screen

Your caitiff heads from Judgment's lifted arm.
Ye pierced the hand that sheltered you from harm;
No mediator now stands in the path—
The nation's vengeance, justice, grief and wrath
May do their worst.

───oo⚬oo───

From MACMILLAN'S MAGAZINE, England.

LINCOLN! When men would name a man
    Just, unperturbed, magnanimous,
Tried in the lowest seat of all,
    Tried in the chief seat of the house—

Lincoln! When men would name a man
    Who wrought the great work of his age,
Who fought and fought the noblest fight,
    And marshalled it from stage to stage,

Victorious, out of dusk and dark,
    And into dawn and on till day,
Most humble when the pæans rang,
    Least rigid when the enemy lay

Prostrated for his feet to tread—
    This name of Lincoln will they name,
A name revered, a name of scorn,
    Of scorn to sundry, not to fame.

Lincoln, the man who freed the slave;
    Lincoln whom never self enticed;
Slain Lincoln, worthy found to die
    A soldier of his captain Christ.

By JOHN NICHOL.

An end at last! The echoes of the war—
  The weary war beyond the Western waves—
Die in the distance. Freedom's rising star
  Beacons above a hundred thousand graves;

The graves of heroes who have won the fight,
  Who in the storming of the stubborn town
Have rung the marriage peal of might and right,
  And scaled the cliffs and cast the dragon down.

Pæans of armies thrill across the sea,
  Till Europe answers—"Let the struggle cease,
The bloody page is turned; the next may be
  For ways of pleasantness and paths of peace!"

A golden morn—a dawn of better things—
  The olive-branch—clasping of hands again—
A noble lesson read to conquered kings—
  A sky that tempests had not scoured in vain.

This from America we hoped and him
  Who ruled her "in the spirit of his creed."
Does the hope last when all our eyes are dim,
  As history records her darkest deed?

The pilot of his people through the strife,
  With his strong purpose turning scorn to praise,
E'en at the close of battle reft of life,
  And fair inheritance of quiet days.

Defeat and triumph found him calm and just,
  He showed how clemency should temper power,
And dying left to future times in trust
  The memory of his brief victorious hour.

O'ermastered by the irony of fate,
  The last and greatest martyr of his cause;
Slain like Achilles at the Scæan gate,
  He saw the end, and fixed "the purer laws."

May these endure and, as his work, attest
  The glory of his honest heart and hand—
The simplest, and the bravest, and the best—
  The Moses and the Cromwell of his land.

Too late the pioneers of modern spite,
  Awe-stricken by the universal gloom,
See his name lustrous in Death's sable night,
  And offer tardy tribute at his tomb.

But we who have been with him all the while,
  Who knew his worth, and loved him long ago,
Rejoice that in the circuit of our isle
  There is no room at last for Lincoln's foe.

London Spectator.

By L. M. DAWES.

ALL our land is draped in mourning,
  Hearts are bowed and strong men weep;
For our loved, our noble leader,
  Sleeps his last, his dreamless sleep—

Gone forever, gone forever,
   Fallen by a traitor's hand;
Tho' preserved his dearest treasure,
   Our redeem'd beloved land.
       Rest in peace.

Thro' our night of bloody struggle,
   Ever dauntless, firm and true,
Bravely, gently forth he led us,
   Till the morn burst on our view—
Till he saw the day of triumph,
   Saw the field our heroes won;
Then his honor'd life was ended,
   Then his glorious work was done.
       Rest in peace.

When from mountain, hill and valley,
   To their homes our brave boys come,
When with welcome notes we greet them;
   Song, and cheer, and pealing drum;
When we miss'd our loved ones fallen,
   When to weep we turn aside;
Then for him our tears shall mingle,
   He has suffered—he has died.
       Rest in peace.

Honor'd leader, long and fondly
   Shall thy mem'ry cherished be;
Hearts shall bless thee for their freedom,
   Hearts unborn shall sigh for thee;

He who gave thee might and wisdom,
  Gave thy spirit sweet release;
Farewell father, friend and guardian,
  Rest forever, rest in peace.
    Rest in peace.

By Rev. Dr. D. P. GURLEY.

REST, noble martyr! rest in peace;
  Rest with the true and brave,
Who, like thee, fell in freedom's cause,
  The nation's life to save.

Thy name shall live while time endures,
  And men shall say of thee,
"He saved his country from its foes,
  And bade the slave be free."

These deeds shall be thy monument,
  Better than brass or stone;
They leave thy fame in glory's light,
  Unrival'd and alone.

This consecrated spot shall be
  To freedom ever dear;
And freedom's sons of every race
  Shall weep and worship here.

O God! before whom we, in tears,
  Our fallen chief deplore;

Grant that the cause, for which he died,
  May live forevermore.

DOXOLOGY.

To the Father, Son, and Holy Ghost,
  The God whom we adore,
Be glory as it was, is now,
  And shall be evermore.

THE END

www.ingramcontent.com/pod-product-compliance
Lightning Source LLC
Chambersburg PA
CBHW031906220426
43663CB00006B/794